THE LITTL[barcode]

Restorative Justice Program Design

Published titles include:

The Little Book of Restorative Justice: Revised & Updated,
by Howard Zehr

The Little Book of Conflict Transformation, by John Paul Lederach

The Little Book of Family Group Conferences, New-Zealand Style,
by Allan MacRae and Howard Zehr

The Little Book of Strategic Peacebuilding, by Lisa Schirch

The Little Book of Strategic Negotiation,
by Jayne Seminare Docherty

The Little Book of Circle Processes, by Kay Pranis

The Little Book of Contemplative Photography, by Howard Zehr

The Little Book of Restorative Discipline for Schools, by Lorraine Stutzman
Amstutz and Judy H. Mullet

The Little Book of Trauma Healing, by Carolyn Yoder

The Little Book of Biblical Justice, by Chris Marshall

The Little Book of Restorative Justice for People in Prison,
by Barb Toews

The Little Book of Cool Tools for Hot Topics,
by Ron Kraybill and Evelyn Wright

El Pequeño Libro de Justicia Restaurativa, by Howard Zehr

The Little Book of Dialogue for Difficult Subjects,
by Lisa Schirch and David Campt

The Little Book of Victim Offender Conferencing,
by Lorraine Stutzman Amstutz

The Little Book of Restorative Justice for Colleges and Universities,
by David R. Karp

The Little Book of Restorative Justice for Sexual Abuse, by Judah Oudshoorn
with Michelle Jackett and Lorraine Stutzman Amstutz

*The Big Book of Restorative Justice: Four Classic Justice & Peacebuilding Books
in One Volume,* by Howard Zehr, Lorraine Stutzman Amstutz, Allan MacRae,
and Kay Pranis

The Little Book of Transformative Community Conferencing,
by David Anderson Hooker

The Little Book of Restorative Justice in Education,
by Katherine Evans and Dorothy Vaandering

The Little Book of Restorative Justice for Older Adults,
by Julie Friesen and Wendy Meek

The Little Book of Race and Restorative Justice, by Fania E. Davis

The Little Book of Racial Healing,
by Thomas Norman DeWolf, Jodie Geddes

The Little Book of Restorative Teaching Tools,
by Lindsey Pointer, Kathleen McGoey, and Haley Farrar

The Little Book of Police Youth Dialogue
by Dr. Micah E. Johnson and Jeffrey Weisberg

The Little Book of Youth Engagement in Restorative Justice
by Evelín Aquino, Heather Bligh Manchester, and Anita Wadhwa

The Little Books of Justice & Peacebuilding present, in highly
accessible form, key concepts and practices from the fields of
restorative justice, conflict transformation, and peacebuilding. Written
by leaders in these fields, they are designed for practitioners, students,
and anyone interested in justice, peace, and conflict resolution.

The Little Books of Justice & Peacebuilding series is a cooperative
effort between the Center for Justice and Peacebuilding of Eastern
Mennonite University and publisher Good Books.

THE LITTLE BOOK OF

Restorative Justice Program Design

Using Participatory Action Research to Build and Assess RJ Initiatives

ALISA DEL TUFO AND E. QUIN GONELL
Foreword by Michelle Fine

New York, New York

Contents

Braiding RJ and Participatory Action Research:
Building Cultures of Care and Radical Hope in Schools and Communities

As you read these pages, you will be invited to think about program design and evaluation, rooted in two radical traditions of justice work—restorative justice (RJ) and participatory action research (PAR). Rarely are these two placed in rich conversation and yet of course they are siblings in solidarity. Each brings a deep commitment to epistemic justice recognizing that knowledge grows vibrant and raw in the bodies/consciousness of those most harmed; that empathic listening and repair are essential as we build communities and movements, as we heal and construct knowledge. Both RJ and PAR light a torch to animate fierce accountabilities to name oppression and to ignite radical hope for what could be. With long roots in movements and revolutions in South America, in Maori struggles in Aotearea/New Zealand, in the anti-apartheid struggles of South Africa and traditions of indigenous communities around the globe, RJ and PAR document pain, challenge harm-doing, build wild coalitions for justice, and choreograph new paths forward. Committed to voices unheard and power inequities contested, with anti-racist and decolonizing passions, both approaches appreciate complex intersectionalities, address inconvenient truths and contest hierarchies of power. RJ centers processes of relational accountability and care in knitting communities where harms have accumulated at the hands of the state, capital, occupation, oppression, exclusion, and social or intimate violence. PAR engages a form of bottom-up inquiry, documenting the untold stories of cumulative violence and resistance, revealing both wounds and privilege, anchored resolutely in the conviction: "no research on us without us." Both RJ and PAR rest on the wisdom of those most impacted and the precious belief that fragile solidarities accompany schools and communities toward *just* cultures of accountability, inclusion, and care. Both RJ and PAR offer us rich ways to reenvision program design and program evaluation *with*, not *for*, community members and young people.

Gifted are the hands, and generous are the hearts, that have spun this book into existence. Alisa del Tufo carries a long and storied history of courage/care/radical hope/passion through the domestic violence movement. E. Quin Gonell brings a more brief, but no less dedicated, history as an educator and restorative justice practitioner, grounded in critical race theory, educational justice, participatory praxis, and intergenerational activism in and around schools. In this book they meet and share stories and experiences about both RJ and PAR as they relate to program development and evaluation; readers are invited to bear witness to their journeys and imagine our own. Alisa and Quin have gathered case studies in schools and communities where participants speak, document, analyze, and hug fiercely as they address harms, embrace *just* commitments, and conjure a world-not-yet.

I offer a foreword as someone steeped in critical PAR projects, engaged and en-love with restorative justice as practiced in/through the Montclair public schools, devastated by the current political moment and yet activated at the RJ-PAR hyphen, where a world-not-yet incubates beyond punishment, beyond white supremacy, beyond state violence, beyond intimate violence, beyond misogyny, transphobia, racism, xenophobia, racial capitalism, and beyond binaries, basking in the sunlight of radical participation, healing, and hope. As you design programs and think toward evaluation strategies, you can now stitch in the sweet threads of restoration and participation.

—Michelle Fine
Distinguished Professor of Critical Psychology
and Urban Education, The Graduate Center, CUNY
Cofounding member of the Public Science Project
Visiting Professor at University of South Africa

Chapter 1
Overview

In the past twenty-five years there has been an explosion of programs, projects, and initiatives that use the term "restorative justice." This work grows from an array of practices that were created and used for millennia in cultures around the world and have been adapted by modern societies. The popularity of restorative practices today reflects multiple trends, including the growing awareness of systemic failures and biases in the justice system (e.g., racial, economic, mental health, and gender) as well as "zero tolerance" and other punitive measures adopted in schools. The positive impact of restorative work over the past several decades around the world is making people and systems reflect on the ways these practices can support and enhance justice, community building, and healing.

This renewed interest has generated an array of programs that use restorative ideas and practices in a wide variety of ways. Included are programs as varied as court diversion, juvenile justice initiatives, deeply spiritual circle work, alternatives to campus-based disciplinary practices, national and

1

international truth and reconciliation projects, and tiered restorative work in schools. Some of these programs are designed to address incidences of harm that fall within large systems or in schools where they focus on addressing behavior problems in an effort to diminish overreliance on incarceration, suspensions, and expulsions. There are other experiments in restorative justice that take this work into community settings, racial justice efforts, and initiatives with survivors of intimate partner violence that focus on healing and repair. Recent social movement work that uses mutual aid as a core practice embodies restorative practice as well.

Fania Davis has said that restorative justice is "a justice that seeks not to punish, but to heal. A justice that is not about getting even, but about getting well. A justice that seeks to transform broken lives, relationships, and communities rather than damage them further."[1] The values at the foundation of restorative practices have the potential to be truly transformative. By transformative we mean that they can generate positive and lasting change for the individual, relationships, communities, and systems. To ensure that our programs are securely rooted in these transformative possibilities, it is important that we design, implement, and evaluate them in a manner that promotes the transformative potential of these fundamental values. Without this alignment, we run the risk of calling work restorative when in fact it is a gentler version of the status quo. It is thus important to work toward aligning our theory, values, and practice while working to implement meaningful and effective programs.

We will highlight a method to move toward this alignment, Participatory Action Research (PAR), that is rooted in similar transformative values and is well aligned with restorative practices. PAR embodies the idea that those who are most impacted by a problem are best suited to solve that problem. PAR helps us refocus our gaze on the strengths and assets of our participants and to use those assets to enrich them, their communities, and our work. It levels hierarchy and strengthens relationships and inclusion. PAR affirms that those most impacted have the ideas, expertise, knowledge, and experience that must be at the core of efforts to create, implement, and evaluate the impact of initiatives to make change both at a personal and system level. Participants also have the potential to be leaders when provided with the opportunity and resources to do so. Like restorative justice, PAR is both a set of ideas and methods giving people ways to align values and employ methods that allow our work to have more transformative power; power to not only resolve conflicts and problems but also to address the structures that maintain inequality.

A challenge that goes along with creating and implementing RJ programs is the tendency to focus on outcomes such as behavior change, cost savings, reductions in time spent in court, and reduced suspensions/expulsions. Although not unimportant, these goals are often driven by funders or institutional partners who seek to justify their investment by measurements that are consistent with quantitative analyses of success and failure. These are measurements that cut against the values at the heart of restorative justice which arise from the indigenous roots we claim to be founded in. A question worth asking is: Are these the right things to measure when it comes to restorative justice? In a field where the values of relationship building, healing, accountability, and repair are paramount, it is important to consider what we want to measure and how we do that. Otherwise, we run the risk of being co-opted by the interests of others whose values may not align with ours.

Focusing so much attention on these quantitative results can put our programs at odds with the underlying values of restorative practice. Although these outcomes may be important, they can undermine or short-circuit the deeper and longer-lasting intentions of restorative practices, such as self-reflection, healing, self-determination and agency, accountability, voluntary participation, equity, fairness and justice, the democratization of voice and knowledge, and relationship and community building. This list is filled with concepts that seem outside the scope of traditional forms of evaluation to assess. PAR offers ways to understand and measure these goals so that our work promotes, strengthens, and sustains these values.

In the following chapters we explore ways in which restorative justice/practice and PAR align, how those ideas and values can support the creation and success of restorative programs through design, implementation, and evaluation strategies and offer a preliminary look at how to design a PAR process. A theme running through this book is the importance of centering social justice values and goals in our work, why they are essential for genuine RJ practice, and how PAR, as a method, can help us focus on social justice as we develop and evaluate our RJ programs. We will also discuss specific initiatives for youth that employ Youth Participatory Action Research (YPAR), and we will share tools and resources that can help you move forward in this work.

4

This book is not a detailed, step-by-step guide for developing a PAR process. There are many handbooks available for that, and we reference them at the end of this book. Rather, we are hoping to provide you with the inspiration and concrete reasons to focus on program development and evaluation and to do these important processes within a PAR framework. We use specific case studies to highlight the why, what, and how of these methods as well as share concrete tools that can be adapted to your work. We hope that, by the time you finish this book, you will have a deeper understanding and the practical know-how to use participatory action research as you design, implement, and evaluate restorative programs.

As Kay Pranis said in a training I (Alisa) took with her, "everything we offer here is an invitation, not a directive." Our hope is that you find that these ideas may help to strengthen and deepen your practice.

Chapter 2
Restorative Justice Values and Social Justice

This book is concerned with how we can center and stay true to restorative justice's values and roots through design and evaluation methods that are consistent with and strengthen them. If our restorative work is to live up to its potential to heal and transform individuals, communities, and systems, we must take a hard look at the ways we may be unintentionally reproducing systems of oppression. The first step in this process is to identify those values that we want our work to promote. Paramount among these is social justice in its many forms; values that center equity, inclusion, and the fair distribution of resources and privileges. To honor, promote, and strengthen these values, we need to identify and explore inconsistencies between what we say are those values and how we actually run our programs. In particular, we must deepen our understanding of cultural practices and how we may be appropriating them and the ways in which we allow or excuse powerful actors from institutions and systems. This chapter identifies these values and explores inconsistencies, providing the backdrop for how to do program development and

7

evaluation differently and more consistently with what RJ values are intended to offer to the world.

Social Justice

Today many of us have some awareness of the sexist, classist, and racist views, policies, and practices of the institutions that regulate our society. We can see their impact in the high rates of poverty, incarceration, foster care, homelessness, mental illness, and poor educational outcomes. The protests led by Black Lives Matter focused attention on the extreme powers of law enforcement and policies in place to protect them. Data that came out of research performed on the "school-to-prison pipeline" reinforced similar conclusions that fly in the face of our ideas of justice and fairness. Consider these data that bring the impacts of systemic oppression into sharp focus:

Incarceration[1]
- Black Americans account for 13 percent of the general US population, yet they make up 38 percent of those confined in prison or jail.
- Incarceration rate for Black vs White Americans: 2,306 vs. 450 per 100,000

Poverty[2]
- Overall poverty rate (all people in the United States): 11.4 percent
- White poverty rate (men and women): 8.2 percent
- Women's poverty rate: 12.6 percent
- African American poverty rate: 19.5 percent
- Hispanic poverty rate: 17.0 percent
- Native American poverty rate: 23.0 percent

Child Welfare Cases and Foster Care[3]

- Black children are 13.71 percent of the population, yet 22.75 percent of children in foster care are Black.
- American Indian/Alaska Native children account for less than 1 percent of the population, yet they make up 2.4 percent of children in foster care.
- White children make up 50.5 percent of the population, yet they account for only 44.37 percent of children in foster care.

We believe that the weight of the statistics do not represent the failures of individuals on a grand scale but rather reflect more systemic policies and practices that do not promote equity and well-being in our communities.

Although we are not naive enough to think that in our modern, postindustrial society we can live without large institutions, we are also not jaded enough to accept the ways that many institutions use their power to enforce beliefs that are unjust to so many. It is our belief that these institutions, which many of our RJ programs work with and within, are part of a system that promotes the values of white, male supremacy; systems that originated at a time in our history when White males were in almost complete control of government, law enforcement, banking, foundations, faith communities, child welfare, health care, and education and developed mechanisms to keep it that way. This is the "system" that restorative justice programs and practitioners must think about critically if we are to avoid becoming yet another tool in the maintenance of this control.

We contend that restorative justice is rooted in values of social justice and we can look to the oft-acclaimed indigenous roots of our work. Drawing on indigenous-sourced principles, we hold that restorative justice is:[4]

- **Community-focused**: "People are not simply individuals in society. Everyone owes special obligations to others."
- **Part of a whole**: "Aboriginal teachings speak of all things in the universe as part of a single whole, interconnected through relationships. The whole includes the physical and the spiritual. Realizing the interrelationships among humans, the Earth and the spiritual builds healthy relationships, which are the foundations of a harmonious society."
- **Addressing harms**: "According to traditional teachings, people will always have different perceptions of the truth and the events that occurred. From this perspective, the truth has more to do with each person's reaction to and sense of involvement with the events in question, for that is what is truly real to them. Thus, objectivity is an illusion and the question of the seriousness of the crime a futile one. The focus of justice, then, is to address the harm done and the causes of the wrongdoing, rather than the severity or the details of the offence."

Although there may not have been a concept of "social justice" when these ideas first evolved, they resonate with the contemporary ideas that we claim

10

are at the heart of restorative justice: centering equity and inclusion and promoting the fair distribution of resources and privileges since we cannot have individual and collective well-being without them. Without refocusing on these principles, we cannot say that we are doing restorative justice. It is critical that we do our work with integrity and, as much as is possible, in alignment with a commitment to social justice in ways that address structural oppression along with individual healing. Without this alignment, the unique and transformative power of restorative justice runs the risk of becoming watered down and misses the chance to have the impact it is capable of having on individuals, relationships, communities, institutions, and systems.

In order for restorative justice to become an "authentic, vibrant social justice movement," the Zehr Institute identifies at least six distinctive characteristics that would need to be embodied:

1. Integrating the populations most affected by injustice (e.g., the harmed and the harmdoers, family connections, and community networks) and amplifying their voices and participatory liberation in the process.
2. Resisting widespread, "quick-fix" and/or politically compromised legislation that can often drive institutional co-option and forced uniformity.
3. Insisting on centering and engaging racial and ethnic justice and healing historical harms of colonization and violent oppression in this country and across the world.

4. Determining to make application to transforming personal, social and structural violence and all intersecting relationships that make up the web of human justice.
5. Committing to de-institutionalization, to decentralized organizational structures, and to "bottom-up" justice expressions and processes.
6. Exemplifying shared and emancipatory leadership models and functions.[5]

These characteristics highlight that it is incumbent on the field of restorative justice to interrogate what we do, how we do it, and whose goals we are promoting as our work becomes more and more accepted and mainstreamed.

Inconsistencies between RJ and Social Justice

As a field, restorative justice has not (yet) adequately addressed the weight that racism, inequality, and structural oppression imposes on the people in our communities. Or, for that matter, the privileges that accompany the standing proffered by whiteness, masculinity, academic accomplishment, and institutional affiliation. The systems that restorative justice programs are increasingly aligned with, such as courts, police, and schools, have a long history of promoting, enforcing, and sustaining oppression. Without realizing it, privileged people have created restorative justice programs that reflect the values and expectations of domination. If our work truly seeks to heal, repair, and promote accountability and build community, then we must not focus only on incidents of individual harm but also on the deeper habits, assumptions, and structures that underscore those acts. For example, we cannot measure our success by the number of youths we divert from the courts but rather whether the communities that youth live in promote their dignity, agency, and well-being. Two particular practices within the field reveal inconsistencies between the social justice orientation of RJ and how programs are developed: cultural appropriation and lack of participation of systems-based actors.

Appropriation

One of the ways that dominant groups exert control is to appropriate, benefit from, and take credit for knowledge creation, cultural expression, and experiences that they did not develop. This "cultural imperialism" erases those who came before, their efforts, and contributions, making it seem as if these ideas sprung from thin air. The roots of much restorative practice lie with Indigenous communities around the world and it is important to acknowledge, understand and honor those roots. For those of us in the United States, we owe much to the First Nations of this land. Although among these peoples there is much diversity of tradition and custom, many of the practices we now call "restorative" were developed and nurtured to support and strengthen relationships and community well-being.

There is only so much that modern, non-Native practitioners can truly understand about the traditional Native way of life. Still, it is essential to understand the history and intent of the methods that are now part of "restorative justice" as well as the values and context of the traditions from which they grew. As the field of restorative justice has embraced the metrics, funding, and expectations of institutions that

13

have created and sustained systems of oppression, we must look carefully at whether we need to engage more deeply with the values that are more central to Indigenous cultures and strive to incorporate them into our work.

Non-Native people should also recognize and take responsibility for the ongoing rupture in the lives and traditions of Indigenous peoples and the constant and continuing violation of relationships and agreements that have characterized the past six hundred years of European expansionism, violence, and domination. There is no healing simply from the recitation of a land acknowledgment at the start of our circles, although it is important to include this. Land acknowledgments take on a performative tone when their meaning is not discussed, and action is not included in the practice. Without careful reflection and efforts to include of the values of Indigenous communities in program development and evaluation, our work will be appropriative rather than appreciative.

Developing a practice of awareness and appreciation, seeking to inform and educate those with whom we engage about these roots and the tendency of dominant cultures to obfuscate and erase the past is important to this effort. Finding ways to integrate real, meaningful action is an important way for us to appreciate the gift of these practices as well as to begin the long road of accountability and repair that is necessary. There are also day-to-day decisions we can make that bring attention to and support these communities. These can include collecting donations to and/or providing participants with opportunities to support social justice/anti-oppression efforts, hiring local businesses owned and run by Indigenous people or other people of color to design program material, be our attorneys, accountants, and caterers, be on our boards, and run and staff our organizations.

Exclusion of Institutional Actors

We often think about restorative justice as a set of practices used to facilitate accountability among individuals. This is an important and meaningful way that restorative practices are used. However, as we move toward centering the values of social justice it is vital to involve the institutions and systems that we live with and within—e.g., schools, health care, criminal/legal, faith, and not-for-profit, creative, and community/civic organizations. As we now know from critical race and feminist theory, social structures, cultural norms, and institutions are not neutral, blank slates. They are created by people with specific ideas and values to promote certain behavior and to limit, stop, or punish other behavior.

If the "system" is not part of the conversation, then we end up supporting the same oppressive revolving door that current policies and practices promote. The authors' experience with institutions has underscored this tendency: institutions seek to maintain the status quo, to promote values and practices that are antithetical to Indigenous and social justice values. The reasons for this are varied but include:

1. Institutions promote practices to control individual behavior and avoid addressing larger systemic forces that they themselves are part of.
2. Institutions create procedures and processes for large groups of people and establish

15

general rules that everyone is expected to obey, avoiding nuance or tailored responses.

3. Institutions are operated by people who have been socialized within punitive systems heavily influenced by colonial philosophies that undervalue equity, community, and social justice.

4. Large systems, such as criminal/legal, policing, and educational, are often contractors/funders of restorative justice programs. This means that their goals and the metrics used to measure them are designed to reinforce the systems themselves. This can mean that restorative work done within these systems is hamstrung from the start.

Tackling these issues is not easy or quick. Some strategies for doing this include: seeking funds from outside large institutions so that you can base your work on the real needs of your people and community; finding individuals within systems who are sympathetic to systems change and engaging them in your work; applying pressure through your work to demonstrate what real change could look like; and advocating for political or policy changes that move the needle toward justice.

Promoting Social Justice through PAR

As restorative justice practitioners we know that our roots in indigenous practices and our more recent history reflect an understanding of harm that goes beyond seeing autonomous individuals who require a specific behavior change in order to repair a harm.

We understand that we live in a society and communities with systems that can support or sabotage us, that harm impacts more than just the particular people actually involved, and that healing requires more or even something different than being punished.

In future chapters, we will be sharing ways that PAR can be used to engage institutional leaders, provide opportunities for the people most impacted to be a central part of refreshing our restorative work, and to build collective and community-oriented solutions, all of which promote the values we want to focus on in our restorative justice work. As Fania Davis writes in the early pages of *Colorizing Restorative Justice,* "If the deepest goals of restorative justice are to embrace ubuntu[6] and to work towards creating the 'beloved community' we must be compelled to work in service of transforming these harms by transforming systems."[7] PAR, in the context of program design and evaluation, can provide us with values, ideas, and tools to help us design, run, and evaluate our work so that it generates more justice, equity, and healing.

Core Restorative Justice Values
- *Respect for human dignity*: The underlying philosophy of restorative justice recognizes each human being as valuable and worthy of being respected.
- *Solidarity and responsibility for others*: People are interdependent, interconnected and diverse, and the quality of those relationships is crucial to the well-being and social cohesion of individuals.

(Continued on next page)

- *Justice and accountability*: The focus of restorative justice is on harms that are unjust or wrong. The goal ought to be to alleviate suffering and to reduce the likelihood of further harm.
- *Truth through dialogue*: A central value for participants in restorative processes, especially for victims, who often need to understand what happened, is obtaining truth through dialogue.[8]

—European Forum on Restorative Justice

Chapter 3
Restorative Justice Program Design and Evaluation

Simply put, we do program design and evaluation to make sure that we are helping the people we set out to help in a manner that is faithful to the philosophy and intentions of the guiding principles of our work. We want to ensure, as much as possible, that we achieve the goals that are at the heart of restorative justice, that our practices align with core values, that we have meaningful methods to determine fidelity to those goals and have ways to improve the alignment of our practice, results, and values. We need to design and assess our programs with this alignment in mind. If we see anti-oppression and social justice at the core of our work, then we must articulate and construct our work in a manner that will nurture these results.

Although this sounds straightforward, it is more complicated than it looks. Sometimes, in our effort to get our programs up and running, we focus more on the practices we use and not on the underlying principles that fuel those practices. Just because we do circles or family team conferencing does not mean that we are doing restorative justice. Only when we have understood and articulated underlying values can we determine whether and how well our methods align with those goals and whether our practices are the right ones to achieve them. As the field expands and develops partnerships with large systems, in particular, the criminal/legal and educational systems, it is very important for us to think this through and hold to the values that distinguish our work.

Program design and evaluation are ways to put our vision into action and to continue honing its effectiveness and impact. By doing this, our work has greater potential to be in alignment with our values and not drift or be co-opted away from core goals. In some ways program design and evaluation are related efforts; each providing opportunities to examine the underlying values and goals of our work and, to the best of our abilities, make sure that our people, methods, training, support systems, outreach, accountability measures, funding streams, stated outcomes, public stance, research, and partnerships support the goals and values we have set out to accomplish. If we are serious about our desire to promote social justice, we must consistently include values and action that promote them in all of the work described above. Here, we discuss critical considerations for program design that promote consistency and for evaluation, to assess accomplishments.

Program Design and Evaluation: Twinned Efforts to Support Restorative Values

Program design looks forward, focusing on how we develop and implement a program that has the best chance of fulfilling our core values; values that are rooted in social justice, empathy, relationship building, centering the voices of those who are harmed, meaningful communication, taking responsibility, being accountable, healing, and repairing harm. Although restorative programs talk about these values in their mission statement, they often do not think critically about how they would know if those values were actually fulfilled in their work.

Evaluation, on the other hand, looks back at what we have done to see how it compares with what we said we wanted to do, what else has been achieved, what barriers exist, what improvements need to be made, and what insights are revealed to help us move forward and make those improvements. Evaluation helps us to determine how we are doing and what we need to do to improve or expand our ability to fulfill our goals and the specific outcomes that grow from them. We must think critically about what we really want to measure and evaluate if we want to have programs that are actually true to the values of restorative justice.

What Do We Typically Measure?

Have you ever taken a customer service survey after you called to file a complaint? Are you satisfied with the questions they ask to determine the effectiveness of their services? For example, after you have received the wrong package or taken your car to the dealer for a repair that wasn't done right, or the billing

21

department of your hospital kept charging you for procedures you did not receive? Usually, the questions they ask in the survey are something like: Was the customer service agent friendly and respectful and knowledgeable; Did they try to resolve your concern? Most often, the customer service people themselves are great. However, the questions never seem to address the underlying problem: their delivery system is messed up; the mechanic didn't analyze and fix the problem properly and your car is still a mess; the hospital has their patient IDs crossed, and the bill collection agency doesn't know that. If these surveys were designed with terms that included the concerns of customers you would find a very different set of questions, ones that got to the issues that were important to actually improve their service! This example provides us with a straightforward justification for this book; incorporating the ideas, experience, and voice of participants centers core values and has the power to reframe how our work gets done.

Although many different methods are used to do program development and evaluation, many focus on the practices of an organization and their success in achieving a set of predetermined measures of effectiveness. These outcomes are reflected in data points such as higher test scores, less school suspensions, more meals provided, fewer hospital visits, etc. The weaknesses of standard design and evaluation practices relate to their lack of attention to core values and their integration into methods. For example, if the organization's mission is to end homelessness, is providing shelter beds an adequate way to accomplish this? They are doing a "good" but is it the right or adequate "good"? Providing shelter beds may be an

22

important secondary outcome but does not address the core value of the organization, which might be ending homelessness.

Dominant theories of program design and evaluation have not always been sensitive to the need for integrity between values, practices, and outcomes. To some extent this is because these arise from established organizations such as universities, consulting firms, and foundations that are tied into and support traditional system-based outcomes. Or because folks think that these core values are not important or are not measurable. Sometimes we hear people say "there is no way to measure changes in empathy or feeling heard"—so they default to other outcomes that are easier to quantify and reflect the needs of the systems they represent. However, these measures represent secondary and tertiary outcomes (discussed in more detail later) that are easily countable: such as lower suspension, shelter beds, or recidivism rates. It is important not to confuse these secondary and tertiary outcomes for the core values of restorative practice. These outcomes can result from well-done practices that align with core values, but they are not the core goals themselves. They are outcomes that can result from very un-restorative practices. For example, someone in administration decides that students will no longer be suspended or expelled. These outcomes can be easily accomplished by new rules or changing how "gatekeepers" interpret behavior. We might think this outcome is good, but let's not call a rule change the result of restorative values and let's not make assumptions about the quality of our restorative work because these outcomes have increased.

23

Programs labeled "restorative" do not automatically maintain a restorative vision. That is, processes and outcomes may not be restorative. For example, restitution may be added to incarceration in order to exact more retribution on the offender; restitution would not serve restorative purposes, but retributive ones. Furthermore, a process may not be implemented in a restorative manner. Finally, in the quest for widespread acceptance of a restorative justice system, funding and utilitarian concerns may cloud the underlying principles and values of restorative justice.

Measuring Values, Not Practices

Clearly a challenge we face as restorative justice practitioners is demonstrating that what we do works. To do that we first have to think deeply and critically about what do we mean by "works"? This is an area of some concern for the field as many describe restorative justice in terms of its practices rather than its values, as discussed earlier. The practices we employ are designed to express and implement the values that are at the core of restorative justice and must always be entered in our design and evaluation. Llewellyn and Howse articulate this as part of their RJ conceptual framework using the following explanation:

If we looked only at the results of the evaluations of restorative justice, the only thing that appears to need honing or attention is its practices. As a result, restorative justice is developing as a set of practices rather than as a different way of doing justice. What we need then is an understanding of the theory underlying restorative justice to guide the evaluation of programs and practices.[1]

Taking a step back, let's think through some of the substantive values that we might want to assess. If we focus on the underlying values of restorative justice, we might expect to see measures of the impact on relationships, community-building, communication, equity, empathy, and skills that generate enhanced positive social attitudes and behaviors, to name a few. The experience of being "heard," recognition of underlying factors that influence behavior, acceptance of responsibility for behavior, open and meaningful communication, and appreciation of difference and structural inequalities are also important pieces of what might be assessed. Measures of success could highlight collaborative processes, improvements in communication skills, self-awareness, improved relationships, and the creation of a stronger, positive sense of community, personal sense of value, stronger empathy, and a sense of agency. This point is also emphasized by Llewellyn and House.

> From this it follows that justice processes may be considered "restorative" only inasmuch as they give expression to key restorative values, such as respect, honesty, humility, mutual care, accountability and trust. The values of restorative justice are those values that are essential to healthy, equitable and just relationships.[2]

As we can see, the values described here do not focus on lowering the number of school suspensions or minimizing recidivism. Although these are valid outcomes, they do not reflect the deeper values of restorative justice and cannot be seen as primary outcomes of any program that considers itself restorative.

Core Restorative Justice Values[3]
- *Peaceful social life*: Peace means more than the absence of open conflict. It includes concepts of harmony, contentment, security, and well-being that exist in a community at peace with itself and with its members.
- *Respect*: All people are treated as worthy of consideration, recognition, care, and attention simply because they are people.
- *Solidarity*: This refers to the feeling of agreement, support, and connectedness among members of a group or community.
- *Active responsibility*: This can be contrasted with passive responsibility, which means being held accountable by others.

Theory of Change and Goal Setting

As Chen has argued:

> . . . a standard program evaluation is not very theory driven. Evaluators tend to assess whether a program has achieved the outcomes anticipated. In other words, they typically fail to inquire into the theory of change inherent in the program design and whether the outcomes were achieved because this theory is a valid explanation for what happened.[4]

Key to creating consistency in values among program development, implementation, and evaluation is articulating a theory of change which can be assessed

26

and, in doing so, articulate the primary, secondary, and tertiary goals of the initiative.

In an evaluation process we want to identify our theory of change and assess its effectiveness. A theory of change proposes that incorporating specific restorative values into our practices will result in a particular set out of outcomes, or goals. It answers that question of why we think that our methods will result in our desired goals. By setting out these goals, we are articulating what we believe drives our work and results in our desired outcomes. A theory of change will reflect primary, secondary goals, and even tertiary goals.

Primary goals are the goals that most accurately express our deepest values and represent the "why" of our work. If these are true to the vision of restorative justice, they will fall into the realm of the social justice values discussed earlier as well as others that we discuss frequently such as empathy, healing, and repair.

Secondary goals are what we hope will result from the effective implementation of the primary goals, such as lowering the number of students being sent to in-school suspension. They are important but are not at the heart of RJ work. The link between primary and secondary goals should bear out in the theory of change.

Tertiary goals are not as central as the secondary goals but, like them, they arise from the effective realization of primary goals. They are no less valuable than secondary goals and may impact other parts of the larger system within which restorative work is embedded. These can include things like less time spent for teachers monitoring in-school suspension rooms, fewer days missed of school, and less court time spent on juvenile cases.

Sample Theories of Change

A stronger sense of agency and empathy (primary goal) will lead to fewer crimes being committed (secondary goal) and less people using the court system (tertiary goal).

If we improve someone's feeling of community connection (primary goal), there will be higher rates of school attendance (secondary goal) and fewer students dropping out (tertiary goal).

People will take more control over their health (secondary goal) when they realize the impact it has on family members or the larger community (primary goal) and there will be fewer emergency room visits (tertiary goal).

If values are at the core of restorative justice, why has the focus been on assessing external measures such as arrest, recidivism, suspension, and dropping out, for example? Our experience suggests the following:

- They are easy to measure. Methods already exist within institutions to document and report these measures of success.
- The agenda of large systems drive the goals of the research. Major systems (e.g., police, courts, child welfare, and schools) are evaluated on their ability to achieve lower rates of these measures. They save taxpayers money.

- Few resources are dedicated to evaluation and program design. This includes money and time, two resources that are needed to do effective participatory action research or good restorative practice.

It is clear to many of us who have tried to implement restorative practices within large systems that the goals of our funders (e.g., school or criminal justice systems) are often quite different from the goals of restorative practice. There is growing concern within the restorative justice movement about these very issues.

Finding a program design and evaluation method that is capable of centering and evaluating core RJ values, as primary outcomes, while also acknowledging other, more concrete outcomes has been a challenge for the field. PAR can help restorative justice practitioners design and evaluate our work in a manner that prioritizes our core values and that reframes outcomes and effectiveness in order to document impact in a manner that is not only consistent with our values but moves the field toward its larger social justice goals as well. In our next chapter we will describe Participatory Action Research (PAR) and why we feel this set of practices should be used to develop and evaluate restorative programs. We will spend the rest of this book laying out how we might, as a movement and as individual programs, develop PAR projects that will support our efforts to measure what is truly unique and valuable about restorative justice and our practices.

Chapter 4
What Are PAR
and YPAR?

Participatory Action Research, or PAR, is a term
for the application of research practices that
value and use the deep knowledge people hold
about their lives and experiences and their ideas
about how to make them better. The process results
in the democratization of knowledge, inclusion
and belonging, the diffusion of leadership, and the
development of mechanisms for shared vision and
power. PAR is particularly well suited to support
the core values of restorative practices as both PAR
and RJ use specific practices to focus on efforts
to develop and deepen meaningful relationships,
strengthen empathy, and create change that allows
all parties to feel heard and respected. Because of
this, PAR has the ability to contribute to strengthening the effectiveness of restorative justice initiatives
in ways that promote equity, justice, and previously
discussed restorative values. PAR works to articulate the core values of your restorative practice,
design programs that support those values, and

31

ultimately evaluate whether what you do actually supports attaining those goals.

In this chapter, we introduce you to PAR and YPAR (where Y stands for youth) and explore its consistency with RJ and RP and how it differs from traditional research practices. We believe that PAR offers powerful principles and strategies that can support the efforts of restorative justice to be(come) a social justice movement that promotes the values of social justice and equity.

What Is PAR?

PAR brings those most affected to the foreground of the program development and evaluation process, acknowledging that they are the experts in their own lives. So rather than responding as a "subject" in a process designed by others, those most impacted are involved from the start in determining what questions need to be asked, what methods will be used, and what analysis will be applied to findings. Engagement is not an afterthought, applied after the "experts" have designed the questions, developed the tools, and mapped out the process and stated desired results. In a PAR project, participants, in collaboration with other stakeholders, design and implement the project and analyze the results in order to suggest change strategies. In PAR, constituents are acknowledged for their expertise and celebrated for their knowledge and insights. Constituents who participate in a PAR project have shared power and responsibility for the work and share the resources and credit. So, in addition to formulating the research questions and methods, participants may be paid, named in publications, speak publicly, participate in policy discussions, help to implement findings, and receive "credit" for their experience in school, on résumés, or as a published member of the working group. Like RJ, there is value, meaning, and importance in the process as well as the outcomes.

The PAR-RJ/RP Nexus

PAR provides a framework that keeps a focus on restorative justice's core values, including social justice aims such as assuring equity, dismantling oppressive systems, and supporting positive relationships. PAR itself is liberatory and transformative, meaning that it can disrupt and realign the structures that uphold racism and other systems that harm, marginalize, and disempower some members of our communities more than others. Here we highlight nine points around which PAR and RJ/RP converge.

1. Nothing About Us without Us

This is the hallmark of PAR and key in restorative practices. Just as restorative practice should include and center the voice and participation of those who are harmed and those who caused harm, so PAR centers the voice and participation of those who are most impacted or harmed by social and community problems. When impacted individuals' real experiences are given credibility, the entire conversation shifts in ways that offer authority and agency for those who are often considered "the problem."

2. Diversified Leadership

PAR centers the leadership of people who have traditionally been sidelined or whose ideas, experiences, and values are ignored in mainstream efforts. PAR does not ask people of color or impacted youth to help or co-facilitate a process after a program has been developed. It means elevating, promoting, and providing the conditions that encourage and allow diverse people to lead from the start. PAR challenges dominant cultures to recognize that their privilege brings with it social, cultural, aesthetic, linguistic, and behavioral values that are not shared equally or at all by others. The idea of white objectivity is a clear example of white supremacy as those values are considered by default to be good and true.

3. Inclusion of Outliers
PAR provides a valuable strategy for breaking out of our own echo chamber by inviting and valuing participants who have different points of view. This brings new ideas, insights, and experiences to the process of program design and evaluation. It encourages deep listening and the willingness to compromise and build nuanced solutions. If we are serious about diversifying our work and transforming our communities, PAR calls us to commit to being more inclusive and developing practices that welcome different life experiences, styles, ideas, and outcomes.

4. Patience to Listen
The process of developing and sustaining meaningful, cross-identity/community relationships and the trust needed to make real change takes time and is filled with surprises and complexity. PAR allows for the time and space needed to truly hear, learn, and change, processes that are not quick or linear. Colonizer concepts of time are based on values of efficiency and productivity; they are goal oriented,

transactional, and linear. These are not necessarily bad qualities. However, when applied to efforts to address the weight of hundreds (or millennia) of oppressions or just the sixteen years of a young person who has harmed someone, this is not the proper approach. In fact, it is an approach that only reinforces the idea that there is a "problem" that we can "solve" and then move on from.

5. Solidarity

PAR is a form of solidarity, in that it builds awareness of shared interests, objectives, standards, and sympathies that create a sense of unity between groups. "Solidarity" signifies the ties in a society that bind people together as one. Many of the issues we try to address using restorative practices have deep historical roots and are invisible to those with privilege. These are the cultural and social issues that, as facilitators, leaders, and practitioners of restorative justice, we must learn to identify, acknowledge and be prepared to discuss and change. In addition, it is unrealistic for our small organizations to solve these problems. This is why the concept of solidarity can be so powerful. Solidarity, in our case, means that, although we may not be able to solve systemic oppression, we can identify the problem and build critical consciousness that can bring about a meaningful form of connection and allyship.

6. Trust in the People

Participants who engage in PAR share leadership; diverse forms of leadership will arise and show themselves to be valuable. The fact that new leaders represent diverse parts of the community will increase buy-in and uptake of restorative practices. Other community members will see leaders who look like them, talk like them, and come from communities like their own, who can provide reality checks and credibility in ways that other leaders could not.

Leaders, including leaders in the restorative justice community, can be mistrustful of sharing or handing off leadership to people less seasoned than they are. Sometimes this concern is a reasonable assessment of skills and other times it is fear of losing power and control or misunderstanding other styles of communication and facilitation.

7. Trust in the Process

PAR and RJ both depend on patience and extended processes. Relationships will develop and strengthen, knowledge will be uncovered and shared, empathy will build and overcome mistrust, solutions will be proposed, and actions will be taken while participants are building their own capacity to learn, heal, communicate, and adjust their point of view. This way of working aligns more with the values of indigenous cultures, which have informed RP, than the culture of counting and efficiency that is used so often today in program design and evaluation.

8. The Institution as Participant

The institution—be that a school, a police force, the courts, a hospital, a not-for-profit organization, or a place of worship—should be part of the restorative and/or PAR process. Their inclusion acknowledges that the institution's practices are important to understand and transform the harms that exist. Without someone representing the institution, there will be no chance to have an honest discussion of the policies and systemic barriers that can cause and sustain harms. Often the barriers to healing or change lie within the policies of the institution, as do the behaviors that cause harm and the climate that generates anxiety or fear. Barbara Sherrod says it well in *Colorizing Restorative Justice*:

> I have witnessed those in power advocating for restorative practices while dismissing the restorative idea that the harm done on institutional levels must first be acknowledged, that institutions must hold themselves accountable and that restoration must take place before we can move forward.[1]

This is one of the key challenges we face as a field if we are to be true to our core values and one that undermines much restorative practice that is short sheeted by institutional neglect.

9. Faithful to Core Values

Both restorative justice and PAR are transformative practices that have the potential to remake relationships, communities, and institutions. If our true goal is to strengthen empathy, accountability, build relationships, and repair harm, then we already have the building blocks to strengthen solidarity, diversify leadership, develop strategies, and change historically oppressive structures.

The following table lays out some additional ways that these practices are linked. They show how PAR can support RJ and can help strengthen the core values our work aims to achieve.

RJ	PAR
Focuses on those most impacted by harm who, together, develop the best outcomes to promote accountability and healing.	Community-led process in which people determine solutions to problems by gathering data from their peers, analyzing it, and taking informed action.
Grounded in Narrative	
Telling one's story foundational because restorative practice depends on personal experience, feelings and intentions, which is best shared through narrative.	Stories of individuals and their communities are foundational. PAR asks "what is the story that *you* want to tell?", rather than the story that outsiders or researchers want to tell.
Sharing one's story allows for the telling of strengths and weaknesses, successes and failures. It is complex and nuanced.	Sharing one's story allows for the telling of strengths and weaknesses, successes and failures. It is complex and nuanced.
Dialogue-Based	
Practices are dialogue-based rather than rule-based. They rely on the idea that through honest dialogue and sharing, human beings can develop compassion and make change.	Based on the idea that by tapping the experiences and ideas of those most impacted participants can feel empowered, respected, and that their lives and ideas have meaning.
Democratizes Knowledge and Change	
Those most impacted by harm are the ones to determine the outcome of the restorative process. It is not the state nor a predetermined set of regulations.	Knowledge is forged at the grassroots and shared with allies to build change that aligns with the needs of those most impacted. This process is not top down.
All participants are impacted by the harm as well as the repair. Everyone leaves the process changed.	Knowledge is reciprocal and participants' and allies' knowledge is honored. They work together to make change grounded in the realities of the community.

Critiques of PAR

Of course, not everyone will agree that PAR is a valid approach to designing and evaluating RJ programs. PAR is considered time-consuming, idealistic, and biased. We hope to demonstrate, however, that all design and evaluation is biased and that RJ is an approach to community building and repair that has the capacity to strengthen human relationships and personal agency and creates positive change. We strongly believe that using PAR will help our field course correct and build programs that are true to our history and desired results.

The Question of Objectivity

Some people, especially other researchers and policy makers, criticize PAR for a lack of "objectivity," claiming that centering those who are most impacted is akin to leaving the henhouse under the supervision of the fox. It makes sense for us to take a deeper look at this critique, especially because restorative justice faces similar criticism. How can we trust that someone who has committed harm is sincere about taking responsibility and isn't participating in a restorative process to "get off easy"? How can we believe that a participant's ideas for new program components isn't the result of some self-centered desire?

At one level, PAR questions the sources and legitimacy of knowledge that we accept as "objective." In an era defined by big data and "scientific legitimacy," it can seem heretical to question the nature of data. We are not doubting the need to collect data about things like economic trends or the effectiveness of vaccines. Counting the number of COVID-19 infections during the pandemic has certainly been important in tracking its path. But it is important to think about what objectivity means in the realm of human behavior, emotions, and the impact of systemic and social marginalization and oppression. And, as shared in Chapter 2, traditional understandings of justice and harm call into question our ability to be objective no matter who we are.

The question of objectivity is also impacted by the role that gatekeepers and rule changes can play in defining what we count and define as successful outcomes. For example, if someone wants to show that youth diversion programs are working, guidelines can be changed to increase the number of young people who get diverted so that more youth are kept out of the courtroom. Does this mean that youth have better outcomes or that the rules have been changed? It seems to merely reflect a new set of metrics, not objective results.

PAR affirms the quantum premise that the "observer" has an impact on the act of observation; an idea that is central to modern physics, philosophy and sociology. From Einstein to Foucault and Freire, this idea has had enormous impact on our consciousness:

> PAR posits that the observer has an impact on the phenomena being observed and brings to their inquiry a set of values that will exert influence on the study. . . . On the other hand, PAR draws on the work of phenomenologists who expand the breadth and importance of experience when they argue that humans cannot describe an object in isolation from the conscious being experiencing that object; just as an experience cannot be described in isolation from its object. Experiences are not from a sphere of subjective

reality separate from an external, objective world. Rather they enable humans to engage with their world and unite subject and object.[2]

From this standpoint, PAR embraces the fact that it is not possible to be fully objective.

The PAR approach to evaluation is radically different from the "usual" evaluative process because of the ways in which it centers the voices and perspectives of those most impacted by the phenomena under inquiry. The following table summarizes some other key differences between these very different concepts of design and evaluation.

Traditional evaluation	PAR evaluation
Led by an outside individual or organization.	Led by a team of diverse stakeholders who have firsthand experience with the issues needing improvement and change.
Those who are being evaluated are not part of the development of the evaluation framework.	Those who are most impacted are involved from the beginning in setting the evaluation questions, creating the methodology, implementing the strategy, analyzing the "data," and developing conclusions.
Outside design and evaluation professionals consider themselves to be "objective."	Objectivity is a product of consensus. Diverse stakeholders bring different points of view to every step of the evaluation. Those with lived experience are believed to have more astute and actionable insight into needed change.

(Continued on next page)

41

Traditional evaluation	PAR evaluation
Outside design and evaluation often results in lukewarm uptake due to its lack of attention to how people really live and make change.	Those who design the process and solutions have lived experience and are trusted by other participants, thus inspiring deeper buy-in and impact.
Outsiders, such as funders, state agencies, and political groups, along with program leadership, determine the key evaluation questions and methods.	Those most impacted determine the key evaluation questions, methods, and analysis. The PAR team determines the primary, secondary, and tertiary goals and audiences as well as the best ways to share results.
Final product is a report or article, which may or may not have practical steps for making improvements. Tends to focus on secondary and tertiary outcomes.	Final product is a collaborative action plan that engages multiple layers of stakeholders. Tends to center primary outcomes/root causes as well as secondary and tertiary outcomes.
Quantitative measures are valued. Decisions about whether and how to gather qualitative data and how to analyze it are up to those in charge of the evaluation with a strong emphasis on academics.	Both quantitative and qualitative data is valued and used. The research team of impacted individuals decide what the key questions are, how to gather, analyze, and understand the data.
Resources, such as funding and connections with policy or community leaders, are held by the evaluation professionals.	Resources and community contacts are shared.
Professionals look for publication and credit for their work. Usually, they depart when the work is done.	Participants share credit and are an ongoing part of the organization and/or the community.

(Continued on next page)

Traditional evaluation	PAR evaluation
Conclusions are theoretical and may or may not actually address the real needs of the program or participants.	Conclusions are actionable, and participants feel ownership, which makes the outcomes more sustainable.
Leadership and expertise remain with the professional evaluators.	Skills and leadership are shared, diverse participants learn new skills, and leadership is distributed throughout the process and organization.
The evaluation process tells us what is happening but not necessarily why it is happening.	Process tells us why something is happening and what we can do about it.

From this table it is now easy to see how those who do traditional research may be critical of PAR. It is also our hope that this chart reveals ways in which the values and methods of PAR are similar to and supportive of restorative justice practices and values.

Youth Participatory Action Research (YPAR)

YPAR is the practice of participatory action research with youth. It is an exciting, empowering, and relationship-building set of practices that can change the way adults view youth, youth view adults, schools and other systems view youth, and youth view themselves and each other. It is a practice of liberatory education that incorporates learning, leadership development, and a sense of agency. It can be centered in schools, classrooms, and other youth-serving organizations and systems that can provide the time, space, and resources for this work.

Our education system faces many challenges, particularly related to equity and disparities in educational experiences and outcomes. These manifest in everything from test scores to the abandonment of "extras" such as art and music, zero-tolerance policies, high-stakes testing, and the school-to-confinement pipeline. Although we now know a lot more about who is failing from data gathered through programs such as No Child Left Behind, we don't seem to have found ways to fix it. It is time to engage the experiences of youth in ways that generate knowledge, leadership, and responsibility while transforming power relations, surfacing the passion and experience of youth, and engaging them in meaningful change efforts. YPAR results incorporate the relational values of restorative practices with learning goals of critical thinking and problem solving.

As noted earlier, both PAR processes, including YPAR and restorative practices, demonstrate that there is value, meaning, and importance in the process as well as the outcomes. Youth participants learn and practice skills such as critical thinking, research design, analysis and problem solving, empathy, deep listening, clear communication, negotiation and compromise, patience, and accountability as they work toward the outcomes revealed in the PAR process. For a YPAR project, this may be addressing such school-related issues as dress codes, achievement gaps, equity, and academic content. In the specific context of restorative practice, a YPAR process might explore the experience of student marginalization, behavior issues, bullying, or suspensions. In YPAR and RJ the underlying issues that need to be addressed are often the same; for example, not feeling heard or trusted, being blamed for things outside one's control. This is a reason why these two practices are such good partners as they have similar values, use similar practices, and seek to achieve results that are deeply aligned. As this "work" is accomplished, participants develop the relationships, skills, and insights to address the current problem and to carry forward to address other challenges as they arise. By centering those who are most impacted by issues, both YPAR and youth-focused restorative work have the power to bring about transformative change.

Let's Ask the Kids

In our quest to make our schools and other youth-serving organizations better places to learn and result in more equitable and just outcomes, we might want to ask:

- Who knows what it means to be a student at your school?
- Who understands what the barriers to inclusion and learning are?
- Who can best describe the impact of the learning environment and school culture on behavior and attitude?
- Who can best articulate the social/system pressures that impact learning and behavior?
- Who might have valuable ideas about how to improve the way the school functions?

If we agree that students themselves know some of the answers to these questions, we have taken the first step toward understanding the value of doing YPAR. Obviously, youth are not the only participants in a school community and the other stakeholder groups—staff, teachers, administrators, and caregivers—also have important contributions to make. Most of the time, school policy or change initiatives do not meaningfully include students, their ideas, and their voices. Imagine how different it could be if students were a valued part of developing and answering these questions.

Both RJ and YPAR seek to engage those who are the most impacted—such as students on the margins, those who do not feel welcome, who are failing, or who are not conforming to conduct standards—to participate in a process that will bring about positive change. Engaging students in a YPAR-based critical inquiry into the conditions in their school that limit their well-being can help them imagine how restorative practices can be used to build and strengthen that community. RJ does this through relationship building practices whereas YPAR does this through a series of liberation-based knowledge creation methods. Together they result in action that improves personal and communal learning, belonging, healing, and change.

YPAR and Critical Pedagogy

In the field of evolutionary biology, there is the concept of the common ancestor. What this means is that "multiple species derive from a single ancestral population." In our case, an influential common ancestor for both RJ and PAR is Paulo Freire, a Brazilian educator and philosopher who was a leading advocate of critical pedagogy. He is best known for his book *Pedagogy of the Oppressed*, which is generally considered one of the foundational texts of the critical pedagogy movement. Although his work does not specifically articulate either RJ or PAR, his ideas have been formative for both.[3]

Critical pedagogy is the belief that teaching should challenge learners to examine power structures and patterns of inequality within systems. Critical pedagogy is student/person-centered, dialogic, and democratic, meaning that everyone has important insights and experiences to share, regardless of their social location. Freire contrasts this to the "banking model" of pedagogy where the teacher "deposits" learning into the "empty" student. In critical pedagogy there is an understanding that we can learn and be our best in environments that are relationship based and center our personal narratives as the starting point for learning and action.

One of the thinkers who helps to knit together restorative practice and participatory action research with a laser focus on race, gender, equity and justice is bell hooks.[4] In her work we hear a loud call for a liberation-based education system based on the "practice of freedom" in which students are active participants in and contributors to the work of learning and self-determination. hooks makes the point that "both teachers and students can learn together in a way that no one acquires the kind of power to use the classroom as a space of domination." She also insists that this experience of domination is not restricted to the teacher/student relationship but is also found where there are divisions between the students, particularly around the issues of race, gender, and sexual orientation. In order to create a true learning environment within the classroom and school, she aims to flatten hierarchies and create a sense of community. hooks maintains that the classroom should be a place that is life-sustaining and mind-expanding, a place of liberating mutuality where teachers and students work in partnership.[5]

YPAR also involves learning practices that are valuable to other forms of academic and career development. As students learn how to do research—e.g., code findings, design and analyze a survey, perform an interview, assess key findings, and identify, understand, interrogate, and solve problems—they practice extremely valuable skills that can support other more traditional forms of education and work.

YPAR Case Study

This YPAR project was conducted at a middle school in Burlington, Vermont, that serves a diverse student population. The impetus of the project was a 2017 school district–wide equity assessment that showed stark disparities in punitive discipline being experienced by students of the global majority, students who are neurodivergent, and students receiving free or reduced lunch. Concerned about these findings, district leaders partnered with University of Vermont education researchers who were developing studies to better understand the processes and outcomes of restorative practices within schools. One of the conditions written into the agreement was that measures would be taken to ensure that student voices would be amplified and centered through the use of YPAR to inform future policy decisions related to the work of redressing school-discipline disparities. The YPAR project was initiated in fall of 2018 when the university researchers assigned

(Continued on next page)

---

me (E. Quin Gonell), a doctoral graduate assistant, to partner with a Grade 6 humanities teacher to codevelop a YPAR curriculum unit that would be taught in conjunction with the ongoing social studies curriculum.

As you will see in the following chapter, the first steps of the PAR process encourage participants to work on strengthening team dynamics. For us, this meant that before preparing to formulate well-informed research questions by engaging in discussions about institutional forms of oppression that cause disparities, we needed to use team-building activities to increase trust among the middle-school participants as well as their adult partners. Thus, our first set of lessons included icebreakers and team-building activities, such as building a marshmallow tower and completing a scavenger hunt. Within this phase, we presented simple questions to the team that prompted us to begin reflecting on our own experiences concerning school equity, such as, "What are the things that make me feel like I belong in this school?" and "What would make me feel more welcome at this school?" Discussing student responses to these kinds of questions prompted the team to seek further knowledge about how the rest of the students in the school might respond to such questions. This allowed us to begin to consider what questions, tools, and approaches we might be able to use to find out.

In the next phase, we began to look at the district data showing discipline disparities. See Step

(Continued on next page)

3 in the next chapter for more details regarding this part of the PAR process. For our project, we decided as a team that we needed to spend some time learning about social justice, historical legacies of oppression, and how we can use our core values and research strategies to help interrogate these barriers and develop ways to challenge them. This part of the project was highly focused on developing critical thinking, and some of the tools we used included the Matrix of Oppression,[6] On the Plate: A Story about Privilege,[7] Unequal Opportunity Race,[8] and Take a Seat.[9] These activities were centered on increasing awareness around identity privilege and how certain social identities can help determine what opportunities are or are not made accessible to people from different groups.

These lessons and activities provided the team with a foundational awareness that was essential for analyzing data regarding discipline disparities from a more equity-centered perspective. Given the concerns that the team observed during the data analysis process, the students became fully convinced that to dig deeper, they should turn to their peers from across the school to learn more about what they were experiencing regarding issues of equity. We moved forward by designing a simple preliminary survey to gather data from students across the school. Once this data was collected and analyzed, the team divided into work groups that each focused on addressing a different equity concern that the data suggested

[Continued on next page]

was occurring within the school. The team then agreed on a single research question that would guide what remained of the YPAR initiative: *Is our school a place where all students feel welcome and safe?* With this question formulated, we were now ready to design our data collection tools and begin collecting data. These steps are indicated in the following chapter as Steps 4 and 5, respectively.

As we entered the data collection design phase, the preliminary survey and research questions were used as a basis to draft a shared hypothesis statement: *Our school is not focusing enough on efforts to help all students feel welcome and included.* Each work group adapted the hypothesis to their specific topic by drafting a testable prediction that would inform the drafting of survey items. For example, the students researching racial discrimination predicted, "Students of color at our school are more likely to feel affected by issues related to structural/systemic inequality/injustice within our school," whereas students researching gender discrimination predicted, "Female students and trans students are more likely to feel affected by issues related to structural/systemic inequality/injustice within our school." Each work group's prediction became the centerpiece of their respective survey design efforts, allowing them to form survey items as statements that survey respondents can either agree or disagree with. For instance, the work group researching racial discrimination added the statement, "I have been treated differently by one or more of my teachers because of my race" to

[Continued on next page]

their survey. Once survey questions were ready, all questions were combined onto a single survey that school administrators agreed to help disseminate, resulting in an 80 percent response rate. Our team was then able to generate preliminary findings and present them to teachers and school leaders before the end of the school year.

Findings from quantitative data corroborated students' concerns regarding racial and gender discrimination. For instance, the work group examining potential race-based issues found that 47 percent of Black students felt that students are discriminating against other students because of their race. They also found that roughly one-third of White students and one-third of Black students agreed that teachers engage in racial discrimination. On the other hand, students studying gender-based issues found that just 21 percent of female-identifying students at their school agreed that adults at the school take action to address gender discrimination. The same work group also found that half of the female-identifying students (49 percent) had seen gender discrimination occur at their school.

The students also conducted qualitative data analysis by coding responses to open-ended survey questions. The first major theme that emerged from qualitative analysis comprised ninety-four comments coded as "students calling for the school to take action to address ongoing race issues." A second theme that emerged comprised sixty-eight comments coded as, "students requesting

(Continued on next page)

increased efforts to raise awareness regarding racial injustice." Given the richness and depth of the data that was generated, it was decided that the following school year, a new YPAR initiative would be implemented to invite a new YPAR team to use the newly collected data as the basis for further research and organizing efforts to improve the school climate.

As we entered the final stages of the PAR process (see Steps 6 and 7 in the following chapter), our efforts resulted in presentations to teachers, the school board, and even at regional academic research conferences held at the University of Vermont. Policy changes resulting from our work also influenced changes made to the school discipline code, informed new initiatives for equity-centered professional development, and an anti-hate rally that marked their school as the first middle school in the state of Vermont to raise the Black Lives Matter flag. School district leaders came to value the work of the YPAR team so dearly that they formed a new position to hire a YPAR coach to train teachers and help implement further YPAR initiatives to amplify student voice at other district schools.

Although this vignette does not demonstrate the application of PAR as a tool to evaluate RJ programs, we would like to note that restorative approaches were regularly applied throughout this YPAR experience. Thus, this case demonstrates a different way that RJ and PAR can complement one another. Given the great value of restorative

(Continued on next page)

practices for building community, establishing trust, fostering collaboration, and holding space for peers in need of emotional support, it felt natural for us to regularly incorporate the use of community and restorative circles throughout the length of the project. It is our observation that by embedding these restorative practices, we were able to greatly enhance the team's ability to communicate openly, form strong teams, and build emotional resilience by holding space during times when members of the team faced harmful forms of resistance while doing YPAR-related fieldwork.

At the core of YPAR, PAR, and restorative practice is the goal of helping everyone feel valued. In our work with youth, in schools, in the justice and child welfare systems, and in almost any other system, young people do not feel heard and valued and do not perceive that their abilities and differences are appreciated and respected. The same can be said for adults impacted by systems. For those interested in interrupting this dynamic, YPAR, PAR, and restorative practice offer relevant intentions that include:

- Everyone's voice is heard
- All are valued
- Empathy and collaboration are key
- Relationships are strengthened
- Agreements are made
- Challenges are addressed
- Change is made

In restorative work, the primary objective is building community through strengthened empathy. In PAR and YPAR, the primary goal is collective critical thinking, engagement in knowledge creation, and problem solving. Using them together is a recipe for success.

Chapter 5
Theory to Praxis:
How to Do PAR Program Design and Evaluation

Program design and evaluation provide pathways for putting a vision into action and continuing to hone its effectiveness and impact. Work conducted in this way has a greater potential to be in alignment with our values and not drift or be co-opted away from our desired goals. In this chapter, we lay out the key organizing questions and steps for a PAR-centered program design and evaluation. We will also provide a window into how two PAR projects worked and what results emerged.

PAR seeks to understand and improve the world by changing it. At its heart it is a collective, self-reflective inquiry that researchers and participants undertake, so they can understand and improve upon the practices in which they participate and the situations in which they find themselves. The reflective process is directly linked to action, influenced by understanding of history, culture, and local context and embedded in social relationships. The process of PAR should be empowering and lead to people having increased control over their lives.[1]

As with RJ, there are certain practices and processes that are central to doing PAR work. It is iterative; that is, the results of one phase will impact the processes of another, and reflection on results is built into the practice. Although the design and evaluation of all programs requires time and resources, a PAR project may require more. To take this on, it is helpful to see it as a process that will provide your organization many positive outcomes for participants, in addition to the development of a new program or evaluation of an existing one. In addition, one approach that some organizations use to launch a PAR process is to do it in partnership with colleges/ universities that may have this expertise or with consultants who can help develop and potentially facilitate a PAR process. There are also training programs (online or in person) where members of your team can learn about developing a PAR project.[2]

All PAR projects are unique. Projects that center and incorporate those who are impacted develop processes, methods, and final products that are specific to the circumstances of your people, program, and community. This next section provides a general set of steps that should guide you through developing and running your project. As you explore these steps, remember that a PAR process is iterative and that one might circle through steps to redo a phase that went before, rather than follow a linear path. For more detailed information, see the recommended resources at the end of the book.

Step 1: Team Foundations

This first phase of the PAR process establishes the PAR team to guide the design/evaluation process.

Establish the PAR Team

Establishing the PAR team is perhaps the most critical step in the process as they are the heart of the work. Similar to facilitating a circle, the team will use a deliberative process to articulate the core questions of the design/evaluation PAR process and will oversee and perform all the other steps described below so they need to have time to invest in working together for several months.

The first consideration is the size and diversity of the PAR team. Although it is best to keep this group fairly small (four to eight people), you should think about how you can get representation from different groups that are important to the success of your work. If you are in a school, for example, you may want to engage a teacher, a student, an administrator (that is, someone with some power), a parent, and someone from a community group you work with. Each one of these people will bring a different point of view as well as connections with different parts of your community.

Some questions to consider as you develop the team include:

1. Who needs to be invited?
2. Who are you leaving out and why?
3. If you could have anyone you wanted to be a part of this process, who would they be and why would their voice be valuable? Is there a way to engage with that person?

4. Are there people you don't want here and why? What will be lost without them?

5. What is the potential impact of your work that will be difficult or impossible to accomplish if they (meaning the people you left out) do not buy in? Are there very specific ways that those individuals could be involved without being part of the PAR team?

Identify a Facilitator

The PAR team facilitator is someone who has skills that are similar to those for circle or facilitated dialogue processes. They should be someone familiar with the organization, the community, and the people the organization is dedicated to helping. This facilitator will provide an anchor for the team process: finding space and setting meetings, providing an overview of work to be done at any meeting, and maintaining communication among the members. Facilitators should address the setting of norms and issues around sharing and rotating group responsibilities such as note-taking, workflow management, record keeping, and other tasks as they come up during the PAR process.

Step 2: Building Team Cohesion and Assessing Resources

This stage of the PAR process focuses on developing a cohesive PAR team, including the establishment of leadership and assessment of the resources that the team will need to conduct the design or evaluation process.

Building Team Cohesion and Leadership

Like restorative practices, in order for your PAR team to be as effective and productive as possible, you need to establish group norms, expectations, and rules of engagement. Participants need to develop these rules in the group itself and decide how they will address issues if members do not follow them. Questions to discuss include:

Division of Labor
1. What are the responsibilities of the team and how can these be shared?
2. Who is going to do which tasks?
3. How will credit be shared?
4. How does the group address conflict and difference in opinion?

Leadership Roles
1. Who will lead the team?
2. Will leadership be shared or rotated?
3. Who will be a spokesperson for the group? How will messaging be developed?

Support, Credit, and Value
1. Are key participants receiving "value" for their work such as money, academic credit, leadership/skill development?
2. What resources are available to share?
3. Given the level of commitment required to accomplish a PAR process, how will team members be supported and/or rewarded?

Work Culture and Expectations
1. What is the work plan and time line to complete the work?
2. How will you maintain accountability and participation over the long haul?

3. How often does your team meet, and what
   are the rules while you are working together?
4. Whose feathers may you ruffle in the
   course of the PAR process and how will you
   address that? For example, if your eventual
   findings are contrary to the ways that leaders
   or others in your community talk about
   problems or solutions or your work finds that
   current solutions are actually exacerbating
   problems, how will you address this in
   a manner that helps your efforts make
   progress and prevents additional roadblocks
   from being put up?

Assessing Available Resources

Before beginning the PAR work, it is important to do
an audit of the resources available to support your
work. Participants will need some compensation,
even if that is academic credit, their name on a publication, or a gift card at the end of the project. Some
well-resourced PAR projects pay their team members,
but this is not always possible. This is real work, and
it undermines the process if one or two team members are being paid (e.g., staff or teachers) and everyone else is working for free. After assessing available
resources, consider the following questions:

1. What other resources are needed—e.g.,
   funds, information/education, transportation?
2. Do you need access to specific expertise?
   For example, help designing a survey, using
   SurveyMonkey, inputting raw data into a
   statistical program, or editing audio or video
   files, to name a few.

3. Do you need access to concrete resources, such as childcare or transportation for team members?
4. Are there project pieces you need to leave behind because you do not have the resources you need?

Once you have gone through this process, you should have a team that has a shared vision for the work and relationships built on trust, has the ability to negotiate and compromise, uses good communication, and understands the resources you need to move on to the next steps.

Step 3: Developing Your Research Questions

PAR is a form of inquiry that asks questions that are rooted in the experiences of the people most impacted by your work. They are not questions that are mandated by outside entities, although these may find their way into a PAR process. During this step, the PAR team will articulate their values and describe possible barriers as well as create the research questions that will guide the design/evaluation work.

Describing Core Values and Barriers

It is important to have extended conversations about the core values of your restorative work. Holding a brainstorming session and using sticky notes to record ideas is a good way to get your team to articulate all the values and practices that are provided by your organization. Remember that the goal of your research question is to dig beneath the secondary and tertiary goals in order to uncover the core values and primary goals of your work. Here are some of the prompts to get your team headed in the right direction:

1. What is your mission?
2. Who are the people you want to help and what do they say they need?
3. What do other organizations want you to do? Do their expectations align with your own? If not, what impact does that have on your work?
4. What are the barriers to achieving your core goals?
5. What are the program's barriers to helping participants achieve those goals?
6. What are you trying to achieve (primary, secondary, and tertiary goals)?
7. Can you articulate how you think that achieving your primary goals will result in succeeding with your secondary and tertiary goals? Remember, this is your theory of change (discussed in Chapter 3), which can be used as a yardstick to assess whether there is consistency between your core values (primary goals) and your secondary/ tertiary goals.
8. Do your answers to these questions reflect what the organization measures now?
9. What are the underlying systemic issues that create barriers to fulfilling your core restorative values?

Developing Your Core Research Question(s)

Once you have discussed the questions above, it is time to craft your core research question(s) that the team is seeking to answer in the PAR process. This question should be the broadest description of the issue you are addressing. Please see the YPAR case study in Chapter 4 for a good overview of how this process works.

In order to create and frame your core question properly, you sometimes need to gather some specific information from your community. This is often an iterative process, because the facts you uncover may impact your understanding of the issues and data that need to be explored. As you saw in the YPAR case example from Chapter 4, the class's process evolved from several questions that were part of their initial discussions and surveys into a single research question that would guide what remained of the YPAR initiative: "Is our school a place where all students feel welcome and safe?"

Let's say that a core question revolves around understanding how can we best help survivors of domestic violence be safe. The process of developing a core question would develop from the exploration of the following questions:

1. What specific information is needed to guide
   your team so that they can develop the
   insight needed to craft your core question?
   For example, policy makers consider having
   an order of protection essential for victims'
   safety, yet many survivors refuse to get them
   because they feel that it will make matters
   worse. Your team may need to inquire
   about issues like this in order to develop
   core questions about challenges faced by
   survivors seeking safety.

2. How do we find a way to understand the underlying barriers from the point of view of the survivors? We can't ask a victim "why don't you leave?" but we may get there by asking questions about their sense of safety and security, their relationships with friends and family, and their experiences with other efforts at safety in order to ultimately understand their needs.

3. How can we understand the issues from the point of view of family and community members? Similar to the above example, family members have insights about the barriers to their loved one's success in protecting themselves. For example, not enough shelter beds, resistance to leaving their job or giving up their home, or uncertainties about how they will be able to care for the needs of dependent children.

The core question should encompass these concerns and then be articulated in affirming language, for example, "How can our community create and sustain ways for survivors to be safe?," not "How do we get domestic violence victims to leave?"

Step 4: Developing Methods and Tools

Once you have developed your core question and clarified some of the information and data you need to gather, you can begin the conversation about the methods you would like to use to collect that information. Most PAR projects use multiple methods to understand the scope of the problem and unearth solutions as different methods are better suited for different types of data collection.

For example, a PAR project focused on schools may start by looking at census data, and team members may read publicly available reports about crime, poverty, unemployment, or school climate, such as the Youth Risk Behavior Survey (YRBS). These data can be used to start discussions in which students and adult allies analyze what the data is saying about them, explore their degree of agreement with findings, and discuss insights, ideas, and strategies to address the issues they prioritize for change. Once some analysis of this is complete, the PAR team might decide to do a community survey and/or series of facilitated dialogues with community members.

During this phase, the PAR team thinks about the methods they want to use, why they would choose them, and how they relate to other methods (for example, using surveys to find key information that then gets incorporated into interviews). This is also the time to think ahead and consider how you want to share your work in a way that aligns with your methods. Finally, consider who your primary audience will be when you share your work and how you can best communicate with them. For example, if your primary audience would be most responsive to a photo show, attend to details such as creating both in-person and online formats and ensuring that your photos will be the correct size and quality. If you are planning to host your presentation on another organization's website, make sure you know the technical requirements before you start your work.

The ultimate goal of this phase is to select the methods that best support your efforts to uncover the information needed to answer your questions. As a result, it is critical for the PAR team to determine which methods are best for your community and will promote the message you want to share. For example, if you are trying to influence policy makers, what methodology do you think will have the biggest impact? Will large numbers of survey results impress them or more detailed oral histories? Is a combination of data the way to go?

Starting with Large Available Data Sets

The methods used in PAR are like matryoshka dolls, the wooden dolls that are nested inside each other. By this we mean that, in most cases, the best way to start your PAR research is with the largest data set that is available and then become more focused as you move through phases. In many cases, a good place to start is with publicly available research, such as evaluation and policy reports, published academic data, news stories, in-house data collection, and census and other data collected by government agencies. Your organization may keep data and/or do reports on its work and others may have done evaluations. These should be reviewed and discussed. These data are interesting because they:

- Are often done repeatedly over time showing trends and comparisons;
- Show the questions/concerns that academics, policy makers, funders, political leaders, and your own organization are interested in;
- Are used for policy decisions and outlay of public and private dollars and reveal where funds are already being spent;

- Reveal what information leaders in your community are using to make decisions;
- Show what people and systems in power are saying and thinking about the people you are working with.

Choosing from Typical Research Methods

There are many research methodologies that are typical in research/evaluation processes that are applicable to PAR. These can be used to address a variety of research questions. Look for support on these methods from people in your community who have used them before.

Surveys and questionnaires: Surveys and questionnaires are good when they are brief, use very clear yes/no or multiple-choice questions, and leave one question for additional comments. Try to get some expert opinions on how to design your survey as creating a survey that will provide you with clarity is challenging. They are often too long or poorly organized. It is important to test your surveys with a small group before you set out to get community members to respond. It is not uncommon to go through several iterations of a survey before it is ready for the public. Always ask whether the person filling out your survey would like to say more about the issue you are addressing! These can be some of the people that you do longer interviews with.

Interviews: Often those who answer surveys are interested in talking more about the issues at hand. In addition, usually there are specific stakeholders who need to be interviewed (e.g., police officers, school principals, board members, and community experts). It is better to do interviews after some data and survey information has been processed to potentially use the interview as a way to explore that information. Interviews are usually structured around a common set of questions that each interviewee answers, providing some common information for your PAR work. There can be time at the end for them to reflect or discuss additional thoughts about the topic at hand. You can record these on a digital recorder or a phone or just write good notes. Doing such an interview with a group of people becomes a focus group, another good PAR method.

Oral History: If you want to more deeply explore people's lives and the ways that the "problem" you are addressing has impacted them, oral histories allow for enormous depth and nuance. If multiple oral histories can be done, themes may arise that impact the work or results. We have seen sensitive interviews with community leaders (principals, law enforcement professionals, etc.) that unearth very important insights that can be genuinely valuable to your work. If allowed by the narrator, the recordings can become a rich source to include in final products through written transcription, audio, or video formats.

Choosing among Creative Approaches

There are numerous creative approaches used in PAR to collect data that go beyond typical research methodologies. For example, setting up "suggestion boxes" in public places or holding conversation circles in the community to share important information and gather ideas and feedback. We offer additional ideas below. As with typical research methods, seek advice about using these methods from people who have used them before. There are examples of some of these methods in the additional resources at the end of the book.

Mapping: What is the geography of your issue? There may be a reason to map the data, problem, or solution. You may be surprised to find that your concerns have a location that is relevant to changes you want to make. Mapping can also be an effective way to share results as well, using online tools.

Photos: A picture is worth a thousand words, and using photography to document the problems you are trying to solve can be a powerful way to demonstrate how participants understand a problem and the meaning of your work. Photo viewers can respond to what they see via feedback discussion sessions or index cards on which they write feedback. PhotoVoice is an established and effective method for doing PAR and there is a tremendous amount of material written about this process.

Performance: Skits and other forms of performance are powerful ways to gather data, especially when the audience is engaged in feedback sessions. YPAR projects lend themselves to performance, as it is a way for young people to communicate their issues without needing to make a "presentation." Performances can travel and be done throughout your community with conversation/dialogue after the show is over. This engages the audience in the process of thinking about the issues that you are also trying to address and can mobilize more support for your work.

The exciting thing about all these methods of data collection is that they can also be used as ways to share information throughout the PAR process. In PAR, the methods and the process of sharing

71

information can all be the means of furthering information sharing and cycling it back into the PAR work itself.

Identifying "Informants"

"Informants" are anyone who has information that you need to inform, or answer, your research question. These are the people who will complete the survey, participate in an interview, or take photos. This could be the school principal or the school bus driver, the mayor or the clerk at family court, the kids hanging out on the corner, or the minister who runs the youth group. It can also include people with specific expertise. Did a university do a study on poverty in your area? Is there an adult who grew up "in trouble" in your area who now mentors kids in trouble? Is there an expert in PAR at a college nearby? These are all possible informants for your PAR project. The critical concern is to figure out who the best informants are for your process and research question and to determine who the best person is to reach out to them.

Step 5: Collecting and Analyzing Data

Now you are ready to gather your data. It is important to set reasonable time lines and expectations here, as this step of the work can take on an endless quality! There are multiple considerations at this phase. For example, do you need two hundred surveys or will fifty be enough? Can a few interviews with key people get you the more nuanced and personal information that you need? Do you have the expertise you need to analyze your data? The PAR team should answer questions such as the following:

Data Collection and Analysis

1. Who will collect your data and who will analyze it?
2. Will those who gather and analyze data be trusted by those expected to share their knowledge and experience?
3. Do you have enough people ready and able to do the work? Is training needed?
4. What program or platform will be used to record and possibly analyze your data? Do you need special software?

Methodological Details

1. How many people will participate in each methodology?
2. Are people using paper surveys? Who will collect and input that data?
3. Are there tablets that can be used for survey taking so that results are immediately tabulated? Surveys on tablets can be linked directly to programs that will record and analyze your data such as SurveyMonkey or Google Forms.
4. Do you need digital equipment for oral histories or photography? Do you need help in editing this material?

Working with Multiple Methods

1. If you use multiple methods (which is suggested for increased validity as a result of data triangulation), how will you learn to develop those methods so that you get the data that you want?
2. How will you understand how different "data sets" work together or don't? Do you need

outside expertise to facilitate this, or is the material you collect transparent enough to draw valid conclusions?

In this phase, the PAR team will typically be collecting and analyzing different types of data simultaneously and may even create new methods for data collection as they work. Think of this phase as a circular, rather than linear, process.

Data should not be thought of as a static object. Data is always in "conversation" or "dialogue" with other data. As we gather and analyze it, we will find that there are places of agreement as well as disagreement across the data. This is exactly what we want it to do! There will be multiple veins to follow as you compare and contrast what different forms of data say to the PAR team. And like a funnel, as you move through this iterative dialogic process, your data will become more focused and clear. It is an exciting process.

Data should be analyzed in waves so that one data set can inform the next stage of data collection. This is part of the iterative strategy of PAR. Questions to consider in this process include:

1. Are there themes that require more detail to make them more understandable? If so, how will you gather that data?
2. Are you getting information that is very different from what you expected? Do you need to rethink your core question or your methods? Do the different messages from the data reveal something important about your work or need for additional inquiry?

3. How do the various forms of data you are looking at "talk to each other"? Are you seeing similar or different information coming from diverse data? For example, are publicly available data saying something very different from what people are saying in their surveys? How do you interpret this?
4. Is there more or different information needed?
5. Have you found that there are other informants who need to be included?
6. What is the data saying about your community and constituents?
7. What is the data saying about systems or organizational services/interventions?
8. How does what you are learning impact what your organization is doing/needs to do?
9. What options exist to create or reimagine the program to address the issues revealed in the data analysis?
10. What are the larger social issues that are being revealed in your research?
11. What can be done about these social issues?

You should begin to think about how the data you collect aligns or not with publicly available results or research. That is, findings may conflict with each other. This means exploring where there are similarities and differences and whether any differences are particularly striking. Conflicting findings may also influence conclusions or generate ideas for next steps in analysis or the "conversation" that occurs between different sets of data. So, for example, when I (Alisa) did a PAR project with survivors of domestic violence, there was data from the child welfare system that blamed them for neglecting the safety of their children. However, when talking with women themselves, I learned that they did everything in their power to protect their children. This contrast created a very important insight into new ways to address this problem.

Analyzing Broad Data (such as publicly available existing data)

Once your team has a grasp on the data that already exists, they will do an "interrogation" of it. This means that they will discuss whether the researchers are asking the right questions, surfacing the right information, and drawing the correct conclusions. This is a good time to consider how your team would go about studying the issue if they were the researchers. For instance,

- What questions would your team like to ask of its community?
- Does your community know that this kind of data is available and what it says?
- How would you interpret this information?
- How would you gather information?
- Do you agree with the conclusions or recommendations drawn by these reports?
- If not, how would you frame questions that could get at the issues your team prioritizes?

This process will set you up for a "conversation" with the other data you are gathering. This dialogue will continue throughout your PAR process and reveal new directions for your work to move forward.

Collecting and Analyzing Medium-Range Data (such as survey data)

Once a PAR team has examined existing data, they will often start collecting new data from their community, starting with a survey or poll that also has a broad reach. Results from the survey may then inform later interview or focus groups. Using surveys can also provide you with so much more than the data you collect. You will engage with people who need to know about your work and your vision for a better community. Below we have included a set of tips or reminders that PAR teams may find helpful as they plan out data collection efforts:

- Set a time frame and total number of surveys you would like to gather.
- Keep it brief! Ten question is a good goal.
- Limit the body of the survey to "closed questions," such as yes/no or multiple-choice questions. They will give you data that can be easily turned into statistics or percentages.
- Include one question at the end where people can express more details and one question asking whether they want to talk more. If they do, ask them for their contact info!
- Decide whom the survey is geared toward. You may need to develop more than one survey for the different groups whose experiences and perceptions you want to better understand.
- Make it asset-based and focused on aspirations or strengths. For instance, what do people want to help them have better

(Continued on next page)

lives? What are the strengths of this group/
community that could be enhanced? What
are the resources needed?
- If you can swing it, send your PAR team out
  into the community to gather survey results.
  It makes your work visible and helps your
  team engage more deeply in the community.
  Consider going to bus/subway stops; pickup
  locations for schools; Laundromats; a school
  cafeteria; a community event; a street corner;
  after religious services, staff meetings at other
  organizations, etc. Have your PAR team set up
  with a clipboard and pencil or tablet. Wider
  conversations will inevitably take place.
- Remember to ask people if they want to get
  more involved. Otherwise, use social media
  to get your survey out or set up times to call
  people to explain the importance of their
  participation.

After you get the desired number of responses to your
survey, your team will review and analyze the results.
If a survey was used in Google Forms or on another survey platform, the platform will tabulate the results for
you and even create pie charts and graphs. Remember
to look over the surveys, especially if you have an open
response at the end. You will learn important things
from what people write on their forms.

Collecting and Analyzing Focused Data (such as interviews and focus groups)

Now you are ready to focus in on a few key issues
that have been highlighted through the steps you

have already taken. Some issues, concerns, and key questions should be rising to the top by now, and the questions you ask in this phase have grown out of what you have learned in previous phases and other forms of data collection. The idea is to get more nuanced and detailed information than what yes/no or multiple-choice responses from the surveys can provide. Here you may want to use focus groups, circles, interviews, or oral histories. Once completed, you will code the recordings from those interactions for major themes and look for patterns in what people tell you. The goal is to understand the overarching themes in the data.

Because you have asked people who took your survey whether they want to get more involved, you should have a group of people with whom your team can engage in these more focused processes. You may also have identified people who you really need to talk with, such as people with specific expertise or experiences. This may include conversations with people who you feel do not support your work. In these more personal contexts, you can share with them the data and potential solutions that you have been uncovering through your PAR work. For example, you might share information about students who drop out of high school because they have become a parent and there is no in-school childcare.

Step 6: Reflection
Once the PAR team has completed the steps above, it is time to reassess the project to ensure that there is continuity between the processes and methods that are chosen, the community involved in the inquiry, and the outcomes you are working toward. If you

need to redo or expand any of your steps, now is the time to do that. If additional expertise is required, pull it in here. Essentially, this is a pause to give your team the chance to determine whether the steps you have taken address the issues you need to understand. You can use a modified circle process to analyze your data by forming questions your group feels are necessary to ask. This might include:

What Have We Learned?
- What does data collected by traditional means, such as publicly available data, tell us about our community? What does that data leave out?
- What conclusions might you draw if you only saw the publicly available data?
- What has surprised you?
- Is there general consensus among the team members on what you are learning or are there significantly different interpretations of the data?

What More Do We Need to Learn?
- What other issues/characteristics need to be understood through data collection and how can we go about that? You may find that you need additional data on an existing issue or you find that there are other concerns you were unaware of and that now need data.
- Who else do we need to talk to?
- Is there significant information that has arisen that requires more exploration?

Program Insights

- What have you learned about your work and ways it needs to change in order to meet the needs of your community and uphold your values?
- Can you see ways that your work does/does not align with your core values?
- Is there continuity between your values, practices, outcomes, and additional needs?
- Do you need to reassess your work, ask new questions, or rethink your goals?

Spending some time at this reflective stage will produce the best outcomes for your research.

Step 7: Sharing Results and Products

Now that you have analyzed your data and reflected on your process, it is time to communicate your results and the action you would like to see happen once your PAR work is shared. In order to make any change happen you need to target the right people with the right message. Discussion of the following questions support you in that effort:

1. Who is your primary audience and your secondary audience? What are the best ways to share your results with them?
2. How will you communicate your results? For instance, through a press conference and media coverage, perform a play, meet with the school board, write a paper, create a video, or do a community presentation? This is related to the question about your

audience and the impact you are seeking to have. Taking a play around to different schools within a district can be an exciting way to share your message and results, especially for other students. Writing a paper that gets published in a peer-reviewed journal will reach a very different audience. Speaking at your city/town council or school board may need different communication strategies.

3. Are there leaders and/or other stakeholders you need to communicate directly with in order to inspire them to embrace your work? Don't forget your funders as part of this audience.

4. Who will communicate your results? Are there members of the PAR team who can do this? Those who have lived experience with the issues you are dealing with are the best spokespeople.

This is your chance to really shine and share your work with enthusiasm and confidence. Show how the people in your community can be thought leaders!

Step 8: Action

Now that you have completed the PAR process, it is time to explore what it is telling you about improvements needed in your program, new programs that need to be created, and/or the systems that impact the lives of your constituents. For example,

1. What specific program changes can you make? How can you achieve this?

2. What specific new programs need to be
   created? How can you achieve this?
3. How will you get the work done? Have you
   built strong relationships during this process
   that can be mobilized to make change? Did
   you connect with potential funders who
   would consider providing financial support
   for your "new" work? Are there partnerships
   that could be strengthened based on your
   findings? Are there campaigns that need
   to be launched in order to make change in
   larger systems?
4. What are the structural barriers that have
   been revealed? How can they be addressed?
   Can action be developed that will change
   those barriers? For example, a march on
   city hall, a press conference or letter-writing
   campaign, or students' engagement at a
   school board meeting?
5. What impact has the PAR process had on
   those involved?
6. Are there ways to create sustainable
   relationships of solidarity from the PAR
   process?
7. If the changes you seek are not going to be
   achievable, can you reframe success in terms
   of changed consciousness and solidarity?

The truth of your findings and the involvement and
voice of your PAR team will create great opportunities for change. Make sure you build in space for cel-
ebration! We don't seem to do enough of this. Enjoy
the work you have done, the relationships you have
made, and the change you have launched.

Case Study: Intimate Partner Violence

This project grew out of an oral history project, that I (Alisa) developed with forty-five survivors of intimate partner violence. In the late 1990s there was a large amount of federal funding going toward shelters and the criminal/legal system, leaving very few other alternatives for women struggling with violence in their homes. Survivor oral histories revealed many reasons that survivors did not use these systems and offered ideas for alternative resources. In fact, most survivors had never sought system-based help, out of fear of unintended consequences. After sharing their oral histories, survivors understood their experiences in different ways, realized the deficits in the systems, and wanted to make changes so that others would not suffer in the ways that they had.

Once the oral history stage of the work was complete, a community-based group of participants did street-level surveying to tap into the experiences and ideas of residents of specific neighborhoods in Brooklyn that revealed their opinions about family violence systems responses and ideas about ways to create new responses. Using crime data as well as results from surveys and discussion groups, a set of ideas were surfaced and honed for creating a network of noninstitutional, community-focused resources for safety and accountability. Survivors testified at the city council and secured funds that were used to seed and sustain these innovative responses to domestic violence.

(Continued on next page)

This PAR project resulted in many community-based, nonpunitive responses to family violence and changes in laws, policies, and community engagement and awareness. This included the development of restorative-based services for survivors (healing circles and community-based safety planning), abusers (accountability and healing circles), and families and the creation of multiple new initiatives based in restorative values (e.g., grassroots education and free training for community professionals, such as teachers, nurses, and clergy).

This PAR project dramatically changed the way that survivors were perceived and their ideas centered in New York City and beyond. The oral histories themselves were listened to, survivor testimony and suggestions for change became the basis for large-scale system change, and other advocates began to consider finding ways to hear "survivor's voice" as a valuable part of their work.

Case Study: Parents, Not Dropouts

In a midsize New England town, a program that works with young mothers who have dropped out of school was interested in doing a PAR project around graduation among the teens in their program. I (Alisa) was asked to facilitate this process, which took about six months. We were able to raise some funds from local faith organizations who were also concerned about these young women

(Continued on next page)

and their children. All the moms were paid; half of their stipend was paid at the beginning of the program and the other half when the project was complete.

There was extensive pushback to this idea from some parts of the community. Local businesses wanted "those people" moved off the streets and even suggested that they were unfit mothers and that their children should be put into foster care. The school district was similarly callous to their plight and essentially said that it was the problem of the mothers themselves to solve. Most of them had become pregnant between the ages of fifteen and seventeen years old.

After meeting with the young moms, we decided to do a PAR process that would start with the young women interviewing each other. The moms listened to and analyzed their stories for themes, and these influenced the development of a survey. The survey was then used by the moms on street corners on the main street of the town and near the pickup sites when parents got their children from school in the afternoon. They collected over two hundred completed surveys. Publicly available data was also explored.

Once the surveying was complete and we reviewed the publicly available data, we entered data from the surveys into a simple online platform that would give us statistics. The moms then discussed the information that was shared through the three different forms of data (interviews, surveys, and public data) and determined that the

(Continued on next page)

school district could make multiple improvements that would allow these young parents to finish their education.

The moms presented their findings to several audiences: the faith groups, the school board, and through the local newspaper. Through this process the school board adopted multiple changes that enabled young parents to continue their education, receive parenting support, and get help securing employment when they were finished with school.

Chapter 6
Applying PAR for Restorative Practices Evaluation

Given how common it is for practitioners and policy makers to become fixated on metrics demonstrating the quantifiable outcomes of restorative initiatives, I (Quin) often find myself having to remind practitioners and decision-makers to reflect upon the values that beckoned them to explore RJ in the first place. Although quantifiable metrics and those related to secondary and tertiary outcomes are important for program evaluation purposes, they tend to pull attention away from the essence of restorative justice, which is about nurturing community and building relationships. When restorative approaches are applied within systems, they tend to shift away from human-centeredness. This issue has been raised in the popular podcast *This Restorative Justice Life* hosted by the founder of Amplify RJ, David Ryan Castro-Harris. Recent episodes engage audiences with questions and topics such as "Can RJ work in systems?" and "RJ as a human process, not a legal one." The podcast is shedding light on the need to explore methods that help keep restorative initiatives grounded in restorative values that are relationship-based, self-reflective, and empowering in nature.

Provided that PAR applies such significant emphasis to inviting participants to help guide assessment efforts and inform the way RJ/RP programs are redesigned to better meet their community's needs, we turn to PAR as a method that can help us achieve that aim. However, examples or guides meant to help restorative program evaluators develop their own PAR-based RP assessments are few and far in between. In response, the current chapter takes a closer look at how practitioners and evaluators in the field are applying these methods through an examination of three studies found in scholarly literature that explore the use of PAR to inform RJ and RP program development, implementation, and evaluation.

Although the literature base comprising studies that assess RP is growing, there remains a dearth of scholarship that applies PAR as a method of RP evaluation. Literature searches on the topic tend to generate studies that employ more traditional research methodologies that examine the experiences of stakeholders to study concepts such as RP buy-in, efficacy, support, and implementation fidelity;[1] RP integration with other transformational pedagogies;[2] and RP outcomes.[3] The case studies that follow highlight how more participatory and action-oriented methods can be applied to 1) explore the development and implementation of RP at a culturally and linguistically diverse school; 2) explore the experiences of racially marginalized youth participating in RP; and 3) support the development of leadership capacities needed to implement RP. The first two case studies showcase the application of PAR methods. The third, however, comprises an action research (AR) process that excludes the "participatory" component. Although we believe the "P" in PAR is critical for program design and evaluation, there are some lessons that can be gleaned by examining and comparing the application of both PAR and AR to inform RJ programming. The chapter concludes with a summary of findings and implications relevant to RP program design and assessment.

Case Study 1: PAR to Evaluate RJ/RP in a Culturally Diverse School

Our first example presents a rigorous three-year study that incorporated participatory tools and methods to introduce, adapt, and support RP in a culturally and linguistically diverse urban elementary school in the San Diego region. The evaluation was specifically intended to explore the experiences of parents, teachers, and students engaging with RP while also examining the extent to which youth participants were empowered to lead.

In this study, the evaluators[4] used a set of frameworks that outline participatory activities that guide engagement with participants including teachers, students, families, graduate students, and other members of the school community throughout the evaluation process. These guiding frameworks are known as the participatory culture-specific intervention model (PCSIM) and the multicultural consultee-centered consultation (MCCC). The PCSIM outlines

91

an eleven-phase, multiyear, recursive, participatory process for developing and evaluating programs aligned with a specific cultural context. As seen in the following table, the eleven phases of the PCSIM are divided into four sequential sections: 1) system entry, 2) model development, 3) program development, and 4) program continuation and extension. Each of the four sections includes its own set of phases that inform the participatory evaluation process. The combined approach provided evaluators with insight into participant perspectives, beliefs, values, and traditions that supported the development of partnerships across cultural groups and informed unique changes relative to the needs of the distinct groups involved in the project.

Eleven Phases of the Participatory Culture-Specific Intervention Model (PCSIM)	
Formative Phases	
1) System Entry *Phase 1:* Existing theory, research, and practice (e.g., exploring and studying the issues affecting the community) *Phase 2:* Learning the culture *Phase 3:* Forming partnerships	**2) Model Development** *Phase 4:* Goal or problem identification (e.g., identifying needs and interests) *Phase 5:* Formative research (e.g., surveying stakeholders) *Phase 6:* Culture-specific theory or model (e.g., identifying and applying frameworks to local realities such as trauma-informed care and RP)

Program Phases	
3) Program Development **Phase 7:** Program design (e.g., participatory generation; collaborative design of new initiatives) **Phase 8:** Program implementation (e.g., natural adaptation involving continuous feedback from participants) **Phase 9:** Program evaluation (e.g., implementing essential changes and elements based on participant feedback and other sources of data)	**4) Program Continuation and Extension** **Phase 10:** Capacity building (e.g., sustainability and institutionalization; building capacity) **Phase 11:** Translation (e.g., dissemination and deployment; presentations at professional and academic conferences)

Throughout the course of the evaluation, participants actively engaged in an iterative process of check-ins to identify goals, design and deliver interventions, and evaluate results to inform further project activities in ways that align with the specific cultures of their school community. Qualitative methods such as interviews and focus groups were applied to explore how the restorative practices were developed and implemented and how stakeholders were engaged and empowered.

Preliminary findings showed that the school's RP program resulted in outcomes directly tied to RJ values, such as greater collaboration with teachers, parents, and students and increased parent and youth leadership in supporting restorative practices. Findings also generated positive outcomes for school and home discipline and fewer discipline referrals. The evaluators also suggest that using the PCSIM and MCCC together to guide the participatory evaluation process may help bridge enduring gaps that exist between the cultures of schools and the cultures of students' homes. Perhaps more relevant for our purposes, this case presents a set of participatory and culturally sensitive guides for evaluators who wish to invite multiple stakeholder groups to collaboratively assess and redesign ongoing RP implementation efforts. Moreover, the assessment tools presented in this study can serve to inform the adaptation of more accessible tools and approaches that can be more practically applied outside academic research contexts.

Case Study 2: YPAR to Assess an RJ Initiative in Service of Underrepresented Youth

This second study set out to apply YPAR to investigate and describe the experiences of fifteen Black male high school students who participated in an RJ program.[5] Given this study's straightforward application of an equity-centered methodology such as YPAR in a context that serves traditionally underrepresented youth, it demonstrates an important contribution to a field of study requiring increased focus on RP approaches that prioritize ethnic and racial equity.

The evaluation invited youth participants to engage in a series of RJ community-building circles designed to help them develop social-emotional learning while collectively exploring in-depth learning outcomes that may result from the community circle processes.

Throughout the course of the project, participants engaged in community-building circles facilitated by the evaluator, who created lesson plans for each circle that were aligned with state teaching and Common Core standards. The circles included topics such as community-building, the value of circles, respect, empathy, self-perception, and personal affirmations. At the end of each circle, participants were invited to complete journal entries to reflect upon shifting personal attitudes, lessons learned, and interactions experienced within the circles. The journal entries, along with interviews, provided data that was central to the evaluator's inquiry into the experiences of Black male students engaging in restorative circles. The findings of the qualitative analysis suggest that relationships are essential to the academic success of the Black male students who participated, and that the community-building circles provided a structure to foster relationship-building. Additionally, the study concluded that the community-building circles provided a safe space for these students to express themselves authentically in ways that improved their self-perception.

This study demonstrates the accessibility of PAR-RP alignment for the purpose of RP evaluation and assessment because it provides a pedagogical model that can be adopted and applied across various contexts; to this end, the evaluator provides the six RJ Community Circle lesson plans included in the study's appendices.

Although not extensively explored in this study, this case opens a window into the transformative potential of PAR as a method of inviting circle participants to play an active role in assessing and improving their restorative practices. By incorporating participants' voices, through the reflective journal responses, as a method of evaluating restorative processes, this study demonstrates how the engagement of study participants as co-investigators can be a core process of PAR.[6] On the other hand, given that the youths' participation during the coding process was limited to member checking, a process where study participants offer their feedback on emerging themes during data analysis, it would seem that the youth participants experienced a reduced degree of involvement through-out the data analysis phase. This circumstance presents a potential oversight that evaluators using PAR should be wary of. Part of what ensures that PAR approaches remain grounded in goals of equity is the emphasis on openly and democratically inviting the engagement of participants in all aspects of the research process.[7] PAR studies that overlook this principal risk perpetuating potentially harmful hierarchical researcher-subject dynamics; a feature that is characteristic of more mainstream research methods, and one that proponents of PAR usually aim to dispel.

Case Study 3: Action Research to Assess Collaboration among Restorative Practitioners

This third case demonstrates an action research (AR) approach that was applied to conduct an evaluation of RJ programming at various sites across a school district. This case does not include the "P" of PAR. However, evaluators with limited access to participants may find the need to apply AR methods, and this case offers distinct lessons that evaluators may find useful.

Using a framework presenting five components of collaboration (governance, administration, organizational autonomy, mutuality, and norms)[8] and the action research model's cyclical process of investigation (Observation; Reflection; Action), a team of evaluators set out to examine the impact of collaboration among restorative justice/practice professionals from across the school district.[9] Their design involved the convening of a group of restorative professionals who were provided with training and a structure to collaborate. The evaluators then studied the group to assess the impact that restorative collaboration might have on their ability to build capacity for restorative initiatives that foster new relationships, ideas, knowledge, and action across the school district. Given this study's framing as an action research project (that is, not "participatory"), the authors did not prioritize participant engagement as coinvestigators throughout the study to the degree that is typically expected in a PAR study. However, the study focused on engaging participants in AR cycles to explore the value of restorative collaboration while examining the links between district-wide collaboration and improved RP implementation. As such, the evaluators incorporated a model providing inclusive and democratic methods to assess RP implementation.

To initiate the AR component of the study, the evaluators gathered approximately thirty stakeholders interested in piloting RP at their respective schools for a one-day restorative conference to learn how to adopt a restorative lens, facilitate restorative conferences, and identify ongoing restorative efforts. The group included administrators, counselors, and school police from eight district schools. At this training, the group engaged in their first AR cycle, during which they were invited to *observe* and *reflect* on their experiences with RP and propose *actions* in response to their observations and reflections. A key result of this first action planning phase was the proposal of a recurring monthly meeting between the stakeholders to collaboratively support the systemic implementation of RP across the district.

The monthly meetings allowed evaluators to facilitate several more action research cycles, which provided the practitioners with a collaborative and generative format for sustaining their work while allowing the evaluators to continue observing and studying the collaborative process. The observation and reflection phases of the second cycle resulted in several additional themes that informed the design of newly proposed actions including creating an online space for remote collaboration, scaling up RP training efforts which included training for youth, and increasing the frequency of smaller meetings and site visits to increase RP knowledge and support skill development.

The collaborative's next meeting was structured as a community-building circle that allowed participants to come into greater awareness of their gratitude for the space, which they came to describe as a source of psychological support. At this third meeting, the collaborative engaged in a final action research cycle that generated further themes to inform the design of actions. For example, newly proposed actions included a commitment to continue holding collaborative meetings throughout the remainder of the school year and into the summer. Additionally, the collaborative committed to addressing inconsistencies and persistent misunderstanding of RP by creating informational videos to be shared across the district.

The evaluators found that by participating in the three RP-themed action-oriented cycles, the collaborative was able to develop leadership capabilities that support the implementation of RP approaches in their respective schools. This case presents the positive impact that these kinds of AR-oriented collaborative meetings can have on the enhancement of the RP work happening at the practitioners' respective schools. As such, this case provides evaluators who are interested in creating platforms to collaboratively design and assess RP programs but lack the access to participants and resources required for PAR, with a more feasible evaluation approach.

Summary

These three case studies provide a window into a world of RP program design and evaluation that is made more accessible, democratic, culturally responsive, and potentially transformative through the application of PAR, YPAR, and AR methods. They also demonstrate a range of possibilities that allow practitioners to attain a level of flexibility that may be necessary when applying PAR to enhance RJ evaluation methods within their unique communities.

Although the first case presents a multifaceted approach that may require significant resources and expertise, it introduces culturally responsive assessment tools such as the PCSIM while presenting methods and procedures that can be adapted and scaled down to be more feasibly applied in the evaluation of smaller-scale RP initiatives. The second case shows the transformative potential of YPAR-RP alignment in efforts to increase understanding of how to better serve underrepresented groups through RP engagement. Finally, the third case provides readers with an example that shows how AR can be used to increase collaboration among school leaders and practitioners working to expand RP efforts across their school district.

We invite readers to review the resources provided at the end of this book to further explore participatory evaluation tools and methods that we view as essential to keeping our restorative practices aligned with our restorative values.

Chapter 7
Conclusion

Our hope is that this book can help to reinvigorate and support our collective belief in the transformative power of restorative justice. We appreciate that there are multiple pressures on our organizations to design and evaluate programs based on values and metrics that are not indigenous to the true lineage of this work. These practical considerations are real and pressure us on a daily basis to privilege secondary and tertiary goals at the expense of the core values that make restorative justice distinctive. However, it is our core values that offer our communities real and practical ways to address our problems without inflicting punishment and shame on each other in ways that have the potential to strengthen well-being, not damage it. If our work is to continue to be a beacon of hope in a world that is divided, divisive, and retributive, we must find ways to keep our light on. PAR is a way to rekindle and shine that light.

It is our hope that readers can see how the PAR-oriented design and evaluation approaches discussed here offer possibilities that enable us to expand our focus from exclusively assessing outcomes such as lowering school suspensions or criminal recidivism to include attention to those outcomes more directly related to deeper values of restorative justice, such as:

- Self-awareness
- Healing
- Empathy
- Accountability
- Self-worth
- Democratization and meaningful participation
- Relationship-building
- Leadership development
- Greater understanding of hidden contexts, such as nuanced power dynamics

Given our personal experiences with the transformative potential of applying PAR methods to inform RJ design and evaluation, we stand firmly in our conviction that there is much to gain from developing a PAR project that will bring our work more deeply in touch with the powerful roots of RJ. As such, we invite others to join us in this exciting exploration. PAR can provide meaningful, engaging forms of knowledge creation that are unique and often challenge traditional evaluation and program design results. PAR will provide community-generated ideas for how to do your best work as well as bring you much stronger connections with your constituents and the larger community.

In addition to everything we have already said, there are other significant benefits that come from a PAR process as well. Examples of such benefits that are aligned with restorative and social justice values include:

- Expanding your circle of connection and influence by inviting and including diverse stakeholders;
- Surfacing leadership from people you may not have known had leadership abilities;
- Centering the real needs, ideas, experiences, and voice of your constituents/participants;
- Strengthening trust and collaboration;
- Creating deeper awareness (both internally and externally) about your mission and work;
- Increasing understanding about restorative justice with diverse stakeholders;
- Deepening everyone's critical thinking abilities;
- Increasing awareness of the value of lived experience in doing all aspects of our work;
- Developing programs that are better aligned with the real needs of your constituents. This may lead to more "success" with secondary/tertiary outcomes as well;
- Demonstrating restorative values at all levels of your organizational practice;
- Developing a policy agenda with stakeholder leadership;
- Identifying new program/project ideas based on PAR recommendations. This can translate into new funding opportunities;
- Creating powerful messaging and spokespeople that grow from the PAR process.

PAR can help restorative justice practitioners to refocus on the more radical possibilities of our work: that as a community of practice we can embrace the messiness of history, take responsibility, resist systemic oppression, right wrongs, be accountable to each other, and work toward healing while promoting insight, compassion, and hope. We hope you will give it a try!

Additional Reading, Resources, and Workbooks

PAR Trainings
- Public Science Project at CUNY (psp.org)
- Shout Hub (shout-hub.eu/sfwd-courses /participatory-action-research)

PAR/YPAR Project Designs (including worksheets and forms)
- Cammarota, J., and M. Fine (eds.) (2008). *Revolutionizing Education: Youth Participatory Action Research in Motion.* New York: Routledge.
- Fine, M. and Torre, Maria Elena (2021). *Essentials of Critical Participatory Action Research.* Washington, DC: American Psychological Association.
- Gonell, E., L. Smith, B. Garnett, and E. Clements (2020). "Practicing Youth Participatory Action Research for School Equity: A Pedagogical Model. *Action Research* 19 (4): 1–23.

- Handbook for Participatory Action Research, Planning and Evaluation (betterevaluation. org/sites/default/files/Toolkit_En_March7 _2013-S.pdf).
- Mirra, N., A. Garcia, and E. Morrell (2016). *Doing Youth Participatory Action Research: Transforming Inquiry with Researchers, Educators, and Students.* New York: Routledge.
- Models for Participatory Action Research and Evaluation (organizingengagement.org/models/ participatory-action-research-and-evaluation/).
- Research for Organizing: A Toolkit for Participatory Action Research from TakeRoot Justice (researchfororganizing.org/).

PAR Tools and Strategies

- Acts of Listening Lab: Oral History/Video (concordia.ca/finearts/research/labs/acts-of listening.html?utm_source=vanity&utm_ campaign=allab).
- Housing Not Handcuffs (housingnothandcuffs .org/).
- How to Design a Survey (bounceinsights.com /how-to-design-a-survey/).
- Morris Justice: A Public Science Project That Highlights Mapping: (morrisjustice.org/process/).
- PhotoVoice (photovoice.org).
- Polling for Justice: A Performance-Based PAR Project (publicscienceproject.org/polling-for -justice-3/).
- Power to Our People Participatory Research Kit: Creating Surveys (powershift.org/sites/default /files/resources/files/creatingsurveys.pdf).

PAR/AR-Based Evaluations of Restorative Approaches (from Chapter 6)

- Darling, J., and G. Monk (2018). "Constructing a Restorative School District Collaborative." *Contemporary Justice Review* 21 (1): 80–98.
- Ingraham, C. L., A. Hokoda, D. Moehlenbruck, M. Karafin, C. Manzo, and D. Ramirez (2016). "Consultation and Collaboration to Develop and Implement Restorative Practices in a Culturally and Linguistically Diverse Elementary School." *Journal of Educational and Psychological Consultation* 26 (4): 354–384.
- Murray, E. J. (2018). "The Power of Caring: A Participatory Action Research Examining Black Male Students' Perspectives in Restorative Justice Community Building Circles" (Publication No. 10825207) [Doctoral dissertation, California State University–Long Beach]. ProQuest Dissertations and Theses Global.

Restorative Justice Resource and Implementation Guides

- Boyes-Watson, C., and K. Pranis (2015). *Circle Forward: Building a Restorative School Community.* St. Paul, MN: Living Justice Press.
- Kidde, J. (December 2017). Whole School Restorative Approach Resource Guide: An Orientation to a Whole-School Restorative Approach and Guide toward More In-Depth Resources and Current Research. Vermont

Agency of Education (education.vermont
.gov/sites/aoe/files/documents/edu-integrated-
educational-frameworks-whole-school
-restorative-approach-resource-guide_0_0.pdf.

Indigenous Roots of RJ

- A Guide to Indigenous Land Acknowledgment
  (nativegov.org/news/a-guide-to-indigenous-
  land-acknowledgment/).
- Lewis, T., and C. Stauffer (eds.) (2021). *Listening
  to the Movement: Essays on New Growth and
  New Challenges in Restorative Justice.* Eugene,
  OR: Cascade Books.
- Native American and Indigenous Initiatives:
  Land Acknowledgment (northwestern.
  edu/native-american-and-indigenous-
  peoples/about/Land%20Acknowledgement.
  html#:~:text=A%20Land%20
  Acknowledgment%20is%20a,Peoples%20
  and%20their%20traditional%20territories).
- Native Land Digital (native-land.ca/).
- Wabanaki Reach (https://www.wabanaki
  reach.org/).

Endnotes

Chapter 1

1. Davis, Fania E. (January 9, 2019). "What's Love Got to Do with It?" *Tikkun.* tikkun.org/whats-love -got-to-do-with-it/.

Chapter 2

1. Prison Policy Initiative. prisonpolicy.org/research /race_and_ethnicity/.
2. Talk Poverty. talkpoverty.org/basics/.
3. National Conference of State Legislators. ncsl.org /research/human-services/disproportionality-and -race-equity-in-child-welfare.aspx.
4. Leung, May. (April 4, 2001). "The Origins of Restorative Justice." Canadian Forum on Civil Justice, www.cfcj-fcjc.org/sites/default/files/docs /hosted/17445-restorative_justice.pdf.
5. Stauffer, Carl. "Restorative Justice—A Movement in the Making?" (2021) in *Listening to the Movement: Essays on New Growth and New Challenges in Restorative Justice.* Eugene, OR: Cascade Books, 168.
6. *Ubuntu* is a South African word that means "I am human because you are." It acknowledges that people are people through other people. *Ubuntu*

is the principle of caring for each other and of being in solidarity. From https://nyrrc.commons. gc.cuny.edu/restorative-justice/.

7. Davis, Fiona. *Little Book of Race and Restorative Justice*. Good Books, 2019.

8. European Forum on Restorative Justice, *Manual on Restorative Justice: Values and Standards for Practice*. p16. https://www.euforumrj.org/sites/default /files/2021-11/EFRJ_Manual_on_Restorative _Justice_Values_and_Standards_for_Practice.pdf.

Chapter 3

1. Llewellyn, Jennifer, and R. Howse. "Restorative Justice—a Conceptual Framework." Schulich Law Scholars. Accessed February 9, 2023. https: //digitalcommons.schulichlaw.dal.ca/scholarly _works/418/.

2. Ibid.

3. Paper by Daniel Van Ness, presented in a plenary session at "The Next Step: Developing Restorative Communities, Part 2," the IIRP's 8th International Conference on Conferencing, Circles and other Restorative Practices, October 18–20, 2006.

4. Chen, Huey. Practical *Program Evaluation: Theory-Driven Evaluation and the Integrated Evaluation Perspective*. (2nd ed.). Sage Publications, 2014.

Chapter 4

1. Valandra, Edward Charles, and Wanbli Waphaha Hoksila. *Colorizing Restorative Justice: Voicing Our Realities*. St. Paul, MN: Living Justice Press, 2020. p55.

2. Baum, Fran, Colin MacDougall, and Danielle Smith (October 2006). "Participatory Action

Research." *Journal of Epidemiology & Community Health* 60 (10): 854–857.

3. Two additional founders are Kurt Lewin, who came to the United States as a Jewish refugee from Nazi Germany during the 1930s and developed the fields of social, organizational, and applied psychology, and Gloria Anzaldúa, who formulated the concept of Borderlands theories. We cannot do justice to their contributions in this short book, but we suggest that you explore their lives and ideas more deeply.

4. Florence, Namulundah (1998). *bell hooks' Engaged Pedagogy: A Transgressive Education for Critical Consciousness*. Westport, CT: Praeger.

5. Specia, Akello[#]and Ahmed A. Osman (2015). "Education as a Practice of Freedom: Reflections on bell hooks," *Journal of Education and Practice* 6 (17): 195–9.

6. Adams, M., L. A. Bell, and P. Griffin (eds.) (2016). *Teaching for Diversity and Social Justice* (3rd ed.). New York: Routledge.

7. Lu, W. (February 13, 2017). "This Comic Explains How Privilege Works." *Bustle*. bustle.com/p/on-a -plate-comic-by-toby-morris-explains-exactly -how-privilege-works.

8. Crenshaw, K., and L. Harris (2010). "Unequal Opportunity Race." African American Policy Forum. https://www.youtube.com/watch?v = EMS_fF0pFzQ.

9. Boyes-Watson, C., and K. Pranis (2015). *Circle Forward: Building a Restorative School Community*. St. Paul, MN: Living Justice Press.

Chapter 5

1. Baum, Fran, MacDougall, Colin, Smith, Danielle (2006). *Participatory Action Research*; *Journal of Epidemiology and Community Health* 60 (10):854–7.
2. Participatory Action Research. Accessed February 9, 2023. https://participatoryactionresearch.sites. carleton.edu/stages-of-par/.

Chapter 6

1. Garnett, B. R., L. C. Smith, C. T. Kervick, T. A. Ballysingh, M. Moore, and E. Gonell (2019). "The Emancipatory Potential of Transformative Mixed Methods Designs: Informing Youth Participatory Action Research and Restorative Practices within a District-Wide School Transformation Project." *International Journal of Research & Method in Education* 42 (3): 305–316.
2. Kervick, C. T., L. C. Smith, B. Garnett, M. Moore, and T. A. Ballysingh (2019). "A Pedagogical Design for Surfacing Student Voice by Integrating Youth Participatory Action Research, Restorative Practices, and Critical Service Learning." *International Journal of Student Voice* 5 (2).
3. Fronius, T., S. Darling-Hammond, H. Persson, N. Hurley, and A. Petrosino (2019). *Restorative Justice in U.S. Schools.* WestEd Justice and Prevention Research Center.
4. Ingraham, C. L., A. Hokoda, D. Moehlenbruck, M. Karafin, C. Manzo, and D. Ramirez (2016). "Consultation and Collaboration to Develop and Implement Restorative Practices in a Culturally and Linguistically Diverse Elementary School." *Journal of Educational and Psychological Consultation* 26 (4): 354–384.

5. Murray, E. J. (2018). "The Power of Caring: A Participatory Action Research Examining Black Male Students' Perspectives in Restorative Justice Community Building Circles" (Publication No. 10825207) [Doctoral dissertation, California State University—Long Beach]. ProQuest Dissertations and Theses Global.

6. Merriam, S. B., and E. J. Tisdell (2016). *Qualitative Research: A Guide to Design and Implementation.* San Francisco: John Wiley & Sons.

7. Gonell, E., L. C. Smith, B. Garnett, and E. Clements (2020). "Practicing Youth Participatory Action Research for School Equity: A Pedagogical Model." *Action Research* 19 (4): 1–24.

8. Thomson, A., J. Perry, and T. Miller (2009). "Conceptualizing and Measuring Collaboration." *Journal of Public Administration Research and Theory* 19 (1): 23–56.

9. Darling, J., and G. Monk (2018). "Constructing a Restorative School District Collaborative." *Contemporary Justice Review* 21 (1): 80–98.

Notes